Cornell Studies in
Industrial and Labor Relations
Number 22

LONGER HOURS OR MORE JOBS?

AN INVESTIGATION OF AMENDING HOURS LEGISLATION TO CREATE EMPLOYMENT

Ronald G. Ehrenberg
and
Paul L. Schumann

**New York State School of
Industrial and Labor Relations
Cornell University**

Cover design by Michael Rider

Library of Congress number: 81-11284

ISBN 0-87546-091-7 (pbk.)

Library of Congress Cataloging in Publication Data
Ehrenberg, Ronald G.
  Longer hours or more jobs?

  (Cornell studies in industrial and labor
relations; no. 22)
    Bibliography: p.
    1. Overtime—United States.   2.Unemployment—
United States.   3. Hours of labor—United States.
I. Schumann, Paul L., 1955–   . II. Title.
III. Series.
HD5111.U5E52   331.25′72   81-11284
ISBN 0-87546-090-9   AACR2
ISBN 0-87546-091-7 (pbk.)

Copies may be ordered from
ILR Press
New York State School of Industrial and Labor Relations
Cornell University
Ithaca, New York 14853

Second printing 1984

To our families,
with love.

CONTENTS

Appendixes

TABLES

ACKNOWLEDGMENTS

This study is the product of two years of research that we conducted under a contract with the Minimum Wage Study Commission. While we are grateful to the commission for its support, the views we express here are solely our own and do not represent the views of the commission or its staff. An earlier, much abbreviated, version of the study appeared in an appendix volume to the commission's final report.

A number of individuals have made contributions to the study that have greatly improved it and warrant recognition. Steven Welch, a senior economist at the commission, was instrumental in helping us obtain several data sets used in our analyses. Our colleagues Eileen Driscoll and William Greene provided us the computer packages necessary to do the complex statistical analyses that we describe in Chapter 7. Numerous colleagues at Cornell and elsewhere have suffered through presentations by us at various professional meetings and university seminars and offered many useful comments; they are too numerous to mention individually. We are especially grateful, however, to Orley Ashenfelter, Daniel Hamermesh, Sar Levitan, and Fred Siskind for reading a draft of the complete manuscript and providing us detailed comments. Patricia Kauppinen expertly typed several drafts of the manuscript. Finally, our editor, Holly Bailey, helped us (successfully we hope) translate technical material into a form that is easily understandable by a wide audience.

Having stated all our debts, we should stress that any errors of omission or commission in this book are strictly our responsibility. Furthermore, the conclusions we reached should not be attributed to any of the individuals we have acknowledged; their views do not necessarily coincide with ours.

1 · HOURS OF WORK LEGISLATION AND THE GROWTH IN OVERTIME HOURS AND FRINGE BENEFITS

It has long been recognized in the United States that excessive use of overtime hours may be partially responsible for continued high rates of unemployment. For although a large proportion of overtime hours is due to disequilibrium phenomena, such as rush orders, seasonal demand, mechanical failures, and absenteeism, much overtime appears to be regularly scheduled. If even a fraction of this overtime could be converted to new full-time jobs, the effect on the unemployment rate might be substantial. For example, in 1977 average weekly overtime hours in manufacturing were 3.4 hours per employee; if one-fifth of this could have been eliminated and converted into new full-time jobs, production worker employment levels would have risen by 1.7 percentage points. As a consequence, proposals have been periodically introduced in Congress to amend the overtime provisions of the Fair Labor Standards Act (FLSA) to restrict the use of overtime. To set the stage for discussing such proposals, a brief history of hours of work legislation is required.

The earliest forms of hours of work legislation in the United States were initiated at the state level, applied to women and children, and had the aim of reducing fatigue and exhaustion (see Commons and Andrews 1920, Paulsen 1959, Phelps 1939, and U.S., Department of Labor 1967). For example, in 1879 legislation regulating maximum hours of work was introduced in Massachusetts, where its supporters claimed that long workweeks were exhausting and caused women to grow prematurely old (Cahill 1932, pp. 106–7). The first hours laws covering men in the private sector were also at the state level and covered occupations in which long workweeks adversely affected third parties or employees themselves. An 1890 Ohio law limited hours of workers who operated trains in the hope that this would reduce railroad accident rates and protect the traveling public. This law was quickly followed by state laws limiting workweeks in mining to protect miners, who were subject to unhealthy and unsafe working conditions (Paulsen 1959, p. 114).

In each of these cases a rationale for the protective labor legislation is found in the fact that the marginal social cost of longer workweeks exceeded the marginal private cost to employers. In the absence of government intervention these divergencies persisted because low family income levels did not permit many women and children the luxury of turning down low wage–long hours jobs, because no good alternatives to the railroads existed for long-range travel and railroad passengers were not always accurately informed about railroad employees' workweeks, and because the limited alternative employment opportunities in mining communities often restricted the occupational choice of individuals in those areas. In each case, then, markets failed, in the sense that compensating wage, or price, differentials did not arise to compensate employees, or third parties, for the full risks they incurred because of long hours of work. The case for government intervention was strong; the only real question is why the legislation took the form of outright restrictions on hours rather than the use of tax or penalty schemes to increase employers' marginal private cost of longer hours.[1]

---

1. The well-known preference of Congress and state legislatures for standards rather than tax-subsidy schemes may reflect only the fact that the majority of their members are lawyers who are comfortable with the standards approach (see Kneese and Schulze 1975; see also Settle and Weisbrod 1978 for a discussion of standards versus tax-subsidy).

Recently Elizabeth Landes (1980) presented an alternative rationale for protective labor legislation. She provides evidence that the effect of state maximum hours legislation in the 1920s was to reduce the average weekly hours and employment levels of foreign-born women, while leaving those of native white women unchanged. She suggests that this implies that support for such legislation, especially by the American labor movement, may have been partially motivated by the well-documented hostility to immigrants that existed during the early 1900s.

Although the average workweek in manufacturing had fallen from 51.0 hours in 1909 to 44.2 hours in 1929, throughout the early 1930s bills were introduced repeatedly in Congress to limit the length of the workweek. While the goal of protecting existing employees from the ills associated with excessive fatigue remained, a second explicit purpose of such legislation was to increase employment by spreading the available work. Ultimately, on June 25, 1938, the Fair Labor Standards Act was enacted. Its overtime provisions established a minimum of one and a half times the regular hourly rate for hours worked in excess of forty-four per week by covered employees for the first year after the act was passed, with the penalty rate beginning after forty-two hours in the second year and forty hours per week thereafter.[2] In its final form, the act covered less than 20 percent of all employees. Since then, employee coverage under the overtime provisions of the act has been expanded until now approximately 59 percent of all employees are covered (table 1.1). The major categories of noncovered employees are supervisory employees, outside salespersons, employees in seasonal industries (including agriculture), state and local government employees, employees in small retail trade and service sector establishments, and some household workers.

Once again, the provisions of the act can be rationalized in terms of the divergence between private and social costs. Even if employers and their employees in the 1930s were satisfied with long workweeks, their private calculations ignored the social costs borne by the unemployed. The time and a half rate for overtime can be thought of as a tax to make employers bear the full marginal social cost of their hours decisions; it was meant to reduce the use of overtime hours and, to the extent that the increased costs do not substantially reduce total manhours demanded, stimulate employment.[3] Furthermore, if employees were not satisfied with long

---

2. Initial drafts of the legislation established outright prohibitions of long hours. The idea of instituting a penalty for overtime instead apparently arose only as a compromise during the late stages of the debate (see Paulsen 1959, Phelps 1939, and Grossman 1978 for legislative histories of the FLSA).

3. As with any other tax designed to correct an externality, such as an effluent tax designed to reduce the emission of pollutants, the time and a half rate for overtime should lead to a reduction in output and some decline in total manhours demanded. One can not, however, evaluate the tax as being bad simply because

4 · Longer Hours or More Jobs?

workweeks during the 1930s but, because of market imperfections, did not have the freedom to choose employment with employers who offered shorter workweeks, the direct payment of the tax to employees who worked longer workweeks can be understood as an attempt to remedy this imperfection.[4]

Although coverage under the overtime pay provisions of the FLSA has increased substantially over the last forty years, the premium itself has remained constant at time and a half. Periodically, proposals have been introduced in Congress to raise the premium to double time. The underlying argument made to support the increase is that while unemployment remains a pressing national problem, the use of overtime hours has increased in recent years. Moreover, the argument follows, since the enactment of the FLSA, the deterrent effect of the overtime premium on the use of overtime has been weakened by the growing share of hiring and training costs, fringe benefits, and government mandated insurance premiums in total compensation. Many of these costs are quasi-fixed or employee related (e.g., vacation pay, holiday pay, sick leave, hiring costs), rather than hours related, in the sense that they do not vary with overtime hours. An increase in these quasi-fixed costs reduces employers' marginal costs of working their employees overtime relative to their costs of hiring additional employees.[5] The growth of these costs, it is claimed, has been at least partially responsible for the increase in overtime and therefore an increase in the overtime premium is required to offset this adverse effect.

Average weekly overtime hours data for manufacturing industries have been collected and published by the Bureau of Labor

---

manhours demanded, and hence output, are lower. This is a necessary consequence of the attempt to correct the externality.

4. Hundreds of court decisions handed down since the FLSA was enacted confirm that Congress had the dual intent of inducing employers to reduce hours of work and increase employment and of compensating employees for the burden of long workweeks. See, for example, Walling v. Youngerman-Reynolds Hardwood Co., Ala. 1945, 65 S.Ct. 1242, 1250; 325 U.S. 419; 89 L. Ed. 1705, *rehearing denied;* 66 S.Ct. 12; 326 U.S. 804; 90 L. Ed. 489.

5. The formal theory of how these quasi-fixed costs influence employers' employment and hours decisions is detailed in a number of places (see, for example, Ehrenberg 1971a and 1971b, Oi 1962, and Rosen 1968 and 1978).

Statistics (BLS) since 1956. Using annual data for all manufacturing, durable manufacturing, and nondurable manufacturing industries, the parameters of equations have been estimated in which weekly overtime hours were specified to be a function of a time trend and the growth in real GNP, the latter to control for cyclical factors (table 1.2). These equations indicate that after controlling for cyclical factors and autocorrelation of the residuals,[6] on average, weekly overtime hours have increased by 0.028 to 0.029 hours each year.[7] Over the twenty-two-year period of the sample, this implies that average weekly overtime hours have increased by 0.616 hours. If all this increase in overtime had been converted to full-time (forty hours per week) jobs, employment in manufacturing would have been 1.5 percent higher [(0.616/40)(100)] in 1977. While this evidence does provide some tentative support for the view that the use of overtime has been increasing, the potential employment increase if it had not increased is a hypothetical *maximum* figure.

Could the increase in the use of overtime have been due to the increase in quasi-fixed nonwage costs that increased the marginal cost of additional employees relative to that of overtime hours? The answer depends upon both the magnitude of the increase in quasi-fixed costs that has occurred and the empirical relationships that exist among these costs, employment, and overtime hours. Em-

---

6. The residuals, in this case, are the part of overtime hours unrelated to time and the growth in real GNP. Autocorrelation occurs when the residual for each year is correlated with the residuals from the previous years. A measure of the extent of autocorrelation is the Durbin-Watson statistic, which can range from 0, denoting the perfect positive correlation, through 2, denoting no autocorrelation, to 4, denoting perfect negative autocorrelation. In table 1.2, the Durbin-Watson statistics indicate the presence of positive autocorrelation. This implies that the ordinary least squares standard errors, which are calculated under the assumption of no autocorrelation, are understated. It is necessary, therefore, to use an estimation procedure that corrects for autocorrelation. The estimates from such a procedure are included in table 1.2. For a more complete explanation of autocorrelation, see Kmenta 1971.

7. Only for the nondurable manufacturing equation, however, is the estimated annual increase statistically significantly different from zero. Moreover, when a quadratic trend term is added to the equation, the upward drift in overtime hours appears to cease sometime between 1971 and 1973. This evidence should therefore be considered only suggestive. It should be stressed, however, that evidence on the trend in overtime hours is not central to the question of whether an increase in the overtime premium would lead to a reduction in overtime hours and an increase in employment.

pirical evidence on the increase in fringes is quite abundant. For example, U.S. Department of Commerce data for the nation as a whole, tabulated in table 1.3, indicate that forms of compensation other than wages and salaries, supplements, rose from 6.2 percent of total compensation in 1956 to 14.7 percent in 1977. These data understate the importance of nonwage items in total compensation because they include holiday, vacation, and sick pay as wages. A more comprehensive measure, although for a more limited sample, comes from the biennial U.S. Chamber of Commerce survey of manufacturing establishments. These data, tabulated in table 1.4, indicate that total fringe benefits rose from 20.3 percent to 37.4 percent of payroll during the 1957–78 period. Both data sets indicate then, an approximate doubling of the share of fringes in total compensation; the increase is due to an increase in employers' legally required insurance payments (social security, unemployment insurance, workers' compensation, etc.) and to the favorable tax treatment of many fringes under the personal income tax, which encourages employers to provide fringes rather than to provide higher wages.[8]

Not all nonwage forms of compensation, however, are independent of employees' hours of work; those that vary with hours do *not* encourage the substitution of hours for employment. Over time, some forms have become "more" hour related. For example, between 1960 and 1978 the Old Age, Survivors, Disability and Health Insurance (OASDHI) maximum taxable earnings level rose from $4,800 to $17,700. This increase caused the fraction of total covered employees with earnings at or above the maximum taxable earnings level to fall from 0.28 at the start of the period to 0.10 in 1977; the fraction of employees for whom the OASDHI tax could be considered not to be hour related declined by over 50 percent. Thus, focusing on the growth of nonwage compensation costs may overstate the increasing incentives employers have to substitute overtime hours for additional employment.

---

8. The BLS also collects data on employer expenditure for employee compensation. Although these data span a shorter number of years, they tell a similar story. For example, between 1959 and 1974, straight-time and premium pay in manufacturing fell from 85.4 to 76.9 percent of total compensation (U.S. Department of Labor, Bureau of Labor Statistics 1973, table 118, and 1977, table 108).

The Present Study

The foregoing arguments and statistics form a backdrop for the present study, which is prompted by a recently proposed amendment to the FLSA, HR 1784. Introduced in February 1979 by Representative John Conyers of Michigan, the bill called for an increase in the overtime premium from time and a half to double time, for the premium to become effective after thirty-five hours a week instead of its current level of forty hours, and for employers to receive the consent of their employees before overtime could be assigned. This study is a comprehensive analysis of the wisdom of instituting the first and third of these proposed changes. Data limitations prevent a complete analysis of the wisdom of the second change; however, it will be briefly discussed in the concluding chapter.

Chapter 2 examines the relationships among the overtime premium, hours of work, and employment. The chapter begins with a critical evaluation of the empirical evidence of previous studies; next, it updates and extends these previous studies; and finally, it discusses the reasons why estimates of the effects of changing the overtime premium derived from the evidence of the original studies and their updated versions are likely to overstate the impact of an increase in the overtime premium on employment.

The next three chapters examine the various factors that would limit the increase in employment of previously unemployed workers induced by an increase in the overtime premium. Chapter 3 discusses the fact that an increase in the overtime premium would lead employers to reduce their overall demand for labor, the possibility of increased moonlighting (holding of second jobs) by existing employees facing reductions in their overtime hours, the possibility that indivisibilities would limit the substitution of new jobs for overtime hours, and the possibility that wages or fringe benefits might adjust in such a manner as to reduce employers' incentives to increase employment. Wherever possible, empirical estimates of the effects of these constraints are presented.

Chapter 4 addresses the issue of whether the skill mix of the unemployed and the skill mix of those working overtime are sufficiently similar to allow any reduction in overtime to be converted into new full-time jobs. Suppose, for example, that all the individuals working overtime were skilled electronics technicians and that all of the unemployed were bakers. It is unlikely that any reduction in the technicians' overtime hours would lead to increased employment. While this example is obviously unrealistic, it illustrates the issue that must be addressed, and the chapter presents data on the extent to which skill mismatches would likely constrain the employment effects of an increase in the overtime premium.

Although analyses of the effects of labor market legislation typically assume that the legislation is fully complied with, noncompliance is always a potential problem. Since an increase in the overtime premium would increase the amount employers save by not complying with the legislation, such an increase might well lead to a reduced compliance rate; this would moderate the actual decline in overtime hours and further reduce the positive employment effect of the legislation. Chapter 5 addresses the noncompliance issue; it summarizes previous estimates of noncompliance with the overtime pay premium, presents new estimates, and attempts to ascertain if noncompliance does appear to be related to the net benefits employers perceive they will receive from complying with the legislation.

Chapter 6 moves away from the potential employment creation effects of an increase in the overtime premium and focuses on the consequences for the income distribution of the existence of overtime hours, the current overtime hours legislation, and proposals to increase the overtime premium. Somewhat surprisingly, virtually nothing is currently known about how compensation for overtime hours influences the distribution of family incomes, or about how changing the overtime premium would alter this distribution. Since policy makers should be concerned with the income distribution consequences of legislation, as well as their efficiency effects, answers to these questions are of utmost importance.

The next chapter evaluates whether, as recently proposed by Representative Conyers, the FLSA should be amended to prohibit mandatory assignment of overtime, so that no overtime could be assigned without prior employee consent. It argues that such an amendment could be considered desirable only if employees who currently are required to work mandatory overtime are not compensated for this "distasteful" working condition by higher straight-time wages or fringe benefits, and it presents empirical estimates of the extent to which such compensating differentials exist.

The final chapter then addresses whether the overtime pay provisions of the FLSA should be amended as proposed in the Conyers bill. It emphasizes alternatives that may be preferable to the Conyers proposal and points out that altering policies other than the FLSA may be a better way to accomplish the goal of stimulating employment growth.

Throughout the study, the discussion has been kept as non-technical as possible, to make it easily accessible to nonspecialists. Technical details are included in several appendixes for interested readers.

TABLE 1.1
Number of Employed Wage and Salary Workers
and Coverage under FLSA Overtime Pay Provisions, 1978
(× 1,000)

Industry	Total	Executives, Administrators, and Professionals[a]	Outside Sales Workers[a]	Nonsupervisory Employees[b]		Percent Subject to Legislation	
				Total	Subject to Legislation	Nonsupervisory Employees	All Workers
	90,730	16,692	2,247	71,791	53,417	74%	59%
Private sector	75,083	10,472	2,247	62,364	50,894	82	68
Agriculture	1,596	78	0	1,518	0	0	0
Mining	894	102	0	792	779	98	87
Contract construction	4,586	460	4	4,122	4,065	99	89
Manufacturing	20,651	2,405	418	17,828	17,505	98	85
Transportation and public utilities	4,908	558	6	4,344	2,652	61	54
Wholesale trade	4,932	701	835	3,396	3,177	94	64
Retail trade	14,702	1,456	132	13,114	9,418	72	64
Finance, insurance and real estate	4,724	683	820	3,221	3,065	95	65
Service industries	16,245	4,029	32	12,184	9,172	75	56
Private household	1,845	0	0	1,845	1,061	58	58
Public sector	15,647	6,220	0	9,427	2,523	27	16
Federal	2,744	518	0	2,226	2,175	98	79
State and local government	12,903	5,702	0	7,201	348	5	3

Source: U.S., Department of Labor, Employment Standards Administration 1979, table 12.
[a] Section 13(a)(1) of the FLSA includes among exempt covered employees "any employee employed in a bona fide executive, administrative, or professional capacity (including any employee employed in the capacity of academic administrative personnel or teacher in elementary or secondary schools) or in the capacity of outside salesmen."
[b] Excluding outside sales workers.

TABLE 1.2

Determinants of Average Weekly Overtime Hours,
1956–77
(standard errors in parentheses)

	All Manufacturing		Durable Manufacturing		Nondurable Manufacturing	
	(1)	(2)	(1)	(2)	(1)	(2)
Ordinary Least Squares						
Time trend[a]	.045*	.036*	.048*	.037*	.040*	.034*
	(.014)	(.012)	(.019)	(.017)	(.009)	(.008)
Change in real GNP		.010*		.012*		.006*
		(.003)		(.004)		(.002)
R^2	.317	.532	.236	.456	.472	.626
Durbin-Watson	.940	.721	.985	.830	.803	.520
Corrected for Autocorrelation						
Time trend[a]	.041**	.028	.044	.028	.038*	.029*
	(.023)	(.020)	(.029)	(.026)	(.015)	(.014)
Change in real GNP		.009*		.011*		.005*
		(.002)		(.003)		(.001)

Source: U.S., Department of Labor 1979.

Notes: *Coefficient statistically significantly different from zero at the 0.05 level of significance, two-tail test.

**Coefficient statistically significantly different from zero at the 0.10 level of significance, two-tail test.

[a] Equals 1 in 1956.

TABLE 1.3

Annual Compensation of Employees,
1957–77
(in billions of current dollars)

Year	Total	Wages and Salaries	Supplements	Supplements as Percent of Total Compensation
1957	256.5	239.3	17.2	6.7%
1959	279.6	258.9	20.6	7.4
1961	303.6	279.5	24.1	7.9
1963	342.9	313.4	29.5	8.6
1965	396.5	362.0	34.5	8.7
1967	471.9	427.5	44.4	9.4
1969	571.4	514.6	56.8	9.9
1971	650.3	580.0	70.3	10.8
1973	797.7	700.9	96.8	12.1
1975	931.1	805.9	125.2	13.4
1976	1,036.8	890.1	146.7	14.1
1977	1,153.4	983.6	169.8	14.7

Sources: U.S., Department of Commerce, Bureau of Economic Analysis 1975, p.6, and U.S., Department of Commerce, Bureau of Economic Analysis 1979, p. S-2.

Notes: Compensation of employees is the income accruing to employees for remuneration for their work.

Wages and salaries consist of the monetary remuneration of employees, including the compensation of corporate officers, commissions, tips, and bonuses, and of payments in kind, which represent income to the recipients.

Supplements to wages and salaries consist of employer contributions for social insurance and other labor income. Employer contributions for social insurance comprise employer payments under old age, survivors, disability, and hospital insurance, state unemployment insurance, railroad retirement and unemployment insurance, government retirement, and a few other minor social insurance programs. Other labor income includes employer contributions to private pensions, health, unemployment, and welfare and privately administered workers' compensation funds; compensation for injuries; and directors' fees.

TABLE 1.4

Fringe Benefits as a Percent of Payroll
in Manufacturing,
1957–78

Year	Employer's Legally Required Payments	Pensions, Insurance	Paid Rest	Pay for Time Not Worked	Other Items	All Fringe Benefits
1957	4.1%	5.8%	2.4%	6.5%	1.5%	20.3%
1959	4.5	6.1	2.7	6.7	1.6	21.6
1961	5.5	6.8	2.8	7.2	1.3	23.6
1963	5.9	6.7	2.9	7.3	1.4	24.2
1965	5.3	6.7	2.7	7.2	1.7	23.6
1967	6.4	7.0	3.0	7.3	1.9	25.6
1969	6.8	7.6	3.1	7.8	1.7	27.0
1971	6.9	9.9	3.5	8.6	1.7	30.6
1973	8.3	10.2	3.5	8.5	1.5	32.0
1975	8.8	11.6	3.7	10.1	1.9	36.1
1977	9.3	12.9	3.6	9.2	2.3	37.3
1978	10.0	12.1	3.5	9.2	2.6	37.4

Source: U.S., Chamber of Commerce, *Fringe Benefits* and U.S., Chamber of Commerce, *Employee Benefits*, various issues.

2 · THE OVERTIME PAY PREMIUM, HOURS OF WORK, AND EMPLOYMENT

Prior Studies

Attempts to estimate the effects of raising the overtime premium from time and a half to double time have exploited the fact that although at any point in time the overtime premium is fixed (legislatively), its value relative to weekly quasi-fixed costs per employee varies substantially across establishments because the level of non-wage benefits varies across establishments (see Ehrenberg 1971a and 1971c, Nussbaum and Wise 1977 and 1978, Solnick and Swimmer 1978, and an earlier unpublished study, Van Atta 1967). These studies used individual establishment data from the 1966, 1968, 1970, 1972, and 1974 Bureau of Labor Statistics *Employer Expenditure for Employee Compensation* (*EEC*) surveys and estimated variants of equations of the form

$$OT = a_0 + a_1R + \mathbf{a_2'X} + \epsilon \qquad (2.1)$$

where *OT* is annual overtime hours per employee, *R* is the ratio of *measured* weekly quasi-fixed nonwage labor costs per employee to the overtime wage rate, and $\mathbf{X}$ is a vector of other variables expected to influence establishments' usage of overtime (throughout this book, bold face letters in equations denote vectors).

All these studies confirm that across establishments, a strong positive relationship exists between the use of overtime hours and the ratio of weekly nonwage labor costs per employee to the overtime wage rate (table 2.1). From these studies one can simulate the effect of increasing the overtime premium on overtime hours, if one assumes that employers fully comply with the legislation and that the change in the premium affects neither straight-time wage rates nor the level of weekly quasi-fixed nonwage labor costs. Moreover, if one also assumes that all the reduction in overtime would be converted to new full-time positions that would be filled by the unemployed, one can simulate what the effect on the employment level would be.

The implied results from such simulations are tabulated in table 2.2. They suggest a *maximum* employment increase in the range of 0.3 to 4.0 percent.[1] It should be emphasized here that these estimates are larger than the actual employment gains that would result since many of the assumptions upon which they are based prove to be invalid. The next three chapters discuss how qualifying the various assumptions would reduce the magnitude of the actual employment effects that might result from the proposed change in the premium.

A number of statistical problems associated with the prior studies suggest, furthermore, that their results should be considered extremely tentative. First, all the studies use ordinary least squares (OLS) to estimate the parameters of equation 2.1. For OLS to produce unbiased and consistent parameter estimates, it is necessary that the dependent variable in the equation be free to take on any value. Since, however, reported overtime hours cannot be negative, and since the limiting value of zero hours frequently occurs, the condition that the dependent variable be free to take on any value is not satisfied. To obtain consistent parameter estimates, it is necessary to use an estimation procedure that explicitly allows for a limited dependent variable, such as Tobit analysis (see Tobin 1958).

Second, it may be argued that to the extent that employers perceive overtime hours as being unavoidable, they will try to reduce

1. These estimates are derived as follows. The decrease in annual overtime hours per employee is given from equation 2.1 by $\Delta OT = a_1 \Delta R$ where ΔR is the change in R caused by the increase in the premium. If the total man-hours demanded remained constant and full-time positions averaging 2,000 hours a year were created, the total number of new jobs created in an industry would be $\Delta E = (-\Delta OT/2,000)E$, where E is the initial industry employment level. In percentage terms, $\%\Delta E = (\Delta E/E)100 = (-\Delta OT)/20$. So in Ehrenberg 1971a, for example, since $\Delta OT = -32$, the resulting simulated $\%\Delta E$ was 1.6 percent.

their overtime costs, and total labor costs, by offering their employees compensation packages that substitute fringes for higher straight-time wages. If this occurs, a positive correlation would be induced between R and OT; however, the direction of causation would run from OT to R. To accurately estimate the effect of R on OT requires a simultaneous equations model in which the determinants of overtime hours and the ratio of nonwage labor cost to overtime wage are simultaneously determined. Only Solnick and Swimmer (1978) have attempted to do this; however, their specification of the nonwage labor cost/overtime wage rate equation was incomplete, as they limited themselves to the variables that were available in the *EEC* survey.

Third, all the studies assumed by their functional form specification that a 10 percent decrease in the weekly quasi-fixed costs F would have the same effect on overtime hours as a 10 percent increase in the overtime wage rate W—that is, they constrained these variables to enter in ratio form: $R = F/W$. None entered the overtime wage rate into the analyses separately to see if this variable had a different effect on hours of work than did the quasi-fixed costs.

Replications and Extensions

To remedy these defects and update the estimates, this study replicates and extends the previous studies, using individual establishment data from the 1976 *EEC* survey. It presents estimates of variants of equation 2.1 of the form

$$\log OT = b_0 + b_1 \log (F/W) + \mathbf{b_2'X} + \epsilon \tag{2.2}$$

and

$$\log OT = c_0 + c_1 \log F + c_2 \log W + \mathbf{c_3'X} + \epsilon. \tag{2.3}$$

Several aspects of the functional forms of these equations and the definitions of the explanatory variables should be noted. First, a log linear model rather than a linear one is used, since this permits the dependent variable to take on negative, as well as positive, values. This is an essential requirement if the desirable statistical properties of OLS are to hold. Second, this specification permits a direct test of whether the overtime wage rate has an independent effect on overtime hours (in which case $c_2 < 0$) and whether the ratio form of the model is correct (in which case c_1 will equal $-c_2$ in equation 2.3).[2]

Third, three different definitions of F and W are used in these analyses. While none exactly captures the desired theoretical variables, a fairly consistent pattern of results across the three definitions should increase confidence in the findings. The first, F_1, W_1, treats all fringe benefits as quasi-fixed costs; although computationally this measure is the easiest to construct, it is flawed because some fringes are hour related. The second, F_2,W_2, includes employer contributions to Old Age, Survivors, Disability, and Health Insurance (OASDHI) as a variable cost. The third, F_3, W_3, includes both employer OASDHI contributions and employer contributions to private funds (health, welfare, vacation, etc.) as variable costs. Since OASDHI contributions are specified as a percentage of salary, this percentage is multiplied by the overtime premium in computing W_2 and W_3 for firms that work their employees overtime. As most contributions to funds are specified as a fixed number of cents per hour, the employers' marginal cost of payments to funds is assumed to be the same for straight-time and overtime hours.

Finally, three specifications of the vector of control variables, **X,** are used. The first includes a dichotomous variable for whether the standard workweek is forty hours or less, the ratio of paid leave to total hours (a proxy for the absentee rate), the proportion of employees with less than one week of annual vacation (a proxy for the experience distribution of the workforce), and a dichotomous variable for union membership. The second specification adds a vector of establishment-size dichotomous variables to this set, while the third also adds a set of dichotomous industry variables. These variables are all intended to control for the other factors that influence the usage of overtime hours, and explanation of why each appears is found in Ehrenberg 1971a.

Table 2.3 presents OLS estimates of selected coefficients of equations 2.2 and 2.3 for a sample of 638 manufacturing establishments; all the manufacturing establishments in the 1976 *EEC* survey

---

2. It would also be desirable to separately estimate the effects of the overtime premium and the straight-time wage on overtime hours. Unfortunately, in the *EEC* survey virtually all firms report their overtime premium to be time and a half so there is not enough variation in the premium to do this.

reported positive levels of overtime hours.[3] Table 2.4 presents similar estimates for the 658 (of 878) nonmanufacturing establishments that reported positive overtime; the problems caused by the zero overtime observations are discussed later.

Most strikingly, the pattern of results differs significantly between the manufacturing and nonmanufacturing industries. Regardless of the definition of F/W or the model specification used, the ratio of quasi-fixed labor costs to the overtime wage rate appears to be significantly positively related to overtime hours in both the manufacturing and nonmanufacturing samples. When equation 2.3 is estimated, however, the relationship between overtime hours and the overtime wage rate vanishes in manufacturing. Indeed, in only one of the nine cases is the relationship negative (table 2.3) as one might expect, and there it is statistically insignificant. In contrast, overtime hours and the overtime wage rate do appear to be significantly negatively related, in most cases, in nonmanufacturing (table 2.4). Put another way, the sum Σ of the overtime wage and quasi-fixed labor cost coefficients, $c_1 + c_2$, is insignificantly different from zero in the nonmanufacturing sector and is significantly different from zero in manufacturing.

How does one resolve these differences in results? The nonmanufacturing results suggest that 2.2 is the correct functional form and that changes in the overtime pay premium do affect overtime hours. In contrast, the manufacturing results suggest that 2.3 is correct and that while increases in the quasi-fixed cost level will, as expected, increase overtime hours, increases in the overtime premium will have *no* effect on overtime hours. One possible explanation is that the variation in the overtime wage rate in the manufacturing sector is somewhat smaller than that in the nonmanufacturing sector; explanatory variables with small variance are less likely to prove to be statistically significant. A second possibility is that due to different technological requirements, the substitutability of employment for hours is more limited in manufacturing. One cannot, however, prove a priori that these are the reasons for the insignificant coefficients in the

---

3. Weighted least square estimates, in which each observation was weighted by its probability of inclusion in the sample (essentially establishment size) were also obtained. Since these estimates were virtually identical to the OLS ones, they are not reported here.

manufacturing case. Accordingly, confidence that an increase in the overtime premium would lead to a reduction in the use of overtime hours in U.S. manufacturing should be substantially reduced.

If one is willing to temporarily ignore this qualification and to assume that equation 2.2 actually is the correct model for manufacturing, one can proceed, as previous studies have, to calculate the percentage decline in overtime hours $\%\Delta OT$, the absolute decline in annual overtime hours ΔOT, and the maximum percentage increase in employment $\%\Delta E$ that would result from increasing the overtime premium to double time from time and a half. These expressions are given, respectively, by

$$\%\Delta OT = (b_1/3) \tag{2.4}$$

$$\Delta OT = (b_1/3)\overline{OT} \tag{2.5}$$

$$\%\Delta E = \Delta OT/20 \tag{2.6}$$

where $\overline{OT}$ is the mean level of overtime initially observed in the sample.[4]

Table 2.5 presents these calculations for both manufacturing and nonmanufacturing establishments. Although the precise numbers differ across model specifications and the various definitions of F/W, these results, in the main, are consistent with those from the previous studies. Annual overtime hours would be predicted to decline by 7.2 to 28.5 percent in manufacturing; this implies an upper-bound percentage increase in employment of 0.5 to 1.5 percent. The nonmanufacturing results are somewhat more optimistic; overtime hours are predicted to decline by 16.6 to 33.8 percent in firms that reported that their employees worked overtime, with a corresponding upper-bound employment gain estimate of 1.0 to 2.3 percent.[5]

---

4. More precisely, these formulae are correct for the specifications that use F_1, W_1 or F_2, W_2. When F_3, W_3 is used, the formulae are a bit more complicated because an increase in the overtime premium from time and a half to double time increases W_3 by less than one-third (since it typically does not change the private employers' holiday, vacation, and welfare fund contributions).

5. It is worth cautioning that if the specification that treats OASDHI payroll taxes as a quasi-fixed cost is excluded, the top of the range of the maximum percentage employment increases falls to 1.0 percent in manufacturing and 1.5 percent in nonmanufacturing. Since most employees earned less than the OASDHI taxable wage base in 1976, payments should be treated as a variable cost by employers. As such, the F_1, W_1 specification is somewhat suspect and may cause the estimate of the maximum employment gain to be optimistic.

Since, however, about 25 percent of the nonmanufacturing establishments initially did not utilize overtime, the estimated upper-bound employment gains would be reduced to about 0.8 to 1.8 percent, which is quite similar to the manufacturing results.

The analyses reported above have been extended in two ways to correct for several statistical problems. First, the fringe-wage ratio F/W has been treated as being simultaneously determined with overtime hours; one might expect that firms that plan to employ a lot of overtime would want to tilt their compensation package towards higher fringes and lower wage rates to make their marginal cost of overtime as low as possible. Although previous researchers attempted to treat the fringe-wage ratio as being endogenous, they confined themselves to using data available in the *EEC* survey (see Solnick and Swimmer 1978). This study generalizes their approach by merging a number of variables for industrywide characteristics, which might be expected to influence the fringe-wage ratio, into each establishment's data record.

These merged variables include measures of the age, sex, race, and ethnic distribution of employees in an industry, as well as the median family income of employees in the industry. The latter variable is meant to capture the effect of individuals' marginal tax rates on their demand for fringes; individuals with higher incomes who face higher marginal tax rates should desire a greater proportion of fringe benefits, most of which are not taxable, in their compensation packages than would individuals with lower incomes. The former set of variables is included to reflect individual tastes for fringes, as well as the ability of a group of employees to agree on a package of fringe benefits. For examples, older workers are likely to have strong preferences for retirement benefits, and industries in which the ethnic mix of the workforce is quite homogeneous are likely to be the ones in which consensus can be reached on a package of benefits.[6] Union status, which is one of the variables available in the *EEC* data, is also important in this regard; unions can serve as the voice by which the preferences of individual workers can be aggregated and made known to management.[7]

---

6. See Lester 1967 for an early discussion of the forces that affect the fringe-wage ratio.

7. Freeman 1978 emphasizes this role of unions and presents empirical evi-

Equation 2.2 has been reestimated by the method of two-stage least squares (2SLS) in the context of a model in which the fringe-overtime wage ratio is simultaneously determined. For comparison purposes, table 2.6 presents both the OLS and 2SLS estimates of the coefficients of log F/W in the hours equations, for each model specification and F/W definition.[8] The most striking finding in this table is that the 2SLS coefficients are always larger than the OLS ones. Although the magnitude of the differential varies across model specifications, it is safe to say that the 2SLS estimates in manufacturing are at least 2.0 to 3.0 times larger than the OLS estimates, while the nonmanufacturing estimates are 1.5 to 3.0 times as large. At first glance this suggests that the upper-bound employment gains reported in table 2.5 may actually be quite conservative, subject of course to the qualification already offered with respect to the manufacturing results. Since the 2SLS results, however, also indicate that increases in overtime reduce the ratio of quasi-fixed costs to the overtime wage in manufacturing, a totally unpredicted result, these findings should not be emphasized too heavily.

The second extension is to include in the analysis the two hundred plus nonmanufacturing establishments that reported that their employees worked no overtime. The analyses so far have excluded them, and as is well known, excluding observations in which zero overtime is worked may lead to biased estimates of the effect of the overtime premium on overtime hours. To obtain unbiased estimates, one should include these observations in the sample and use Tobit analysis (see Kmenta 1971 or any standard econometrics textbook).

Table 2.7 presents estimates of the fringe-wage coefficients from equation 2.1 for the nonmanufacturing establishments using three different samples and estimation methods: OLS estimation over the whole (including zero overtime establishments) sample, OLS estimation using the sample of establishments that reported positive overtime, and finally, Tobit analysis using the entire sample.

---

dence that fringe benefits and the fringe-wage ratio are higher in union than non-union workplaces, other things equal.

8. For the interested reader, the 2SLS estimates of both the annual overtime and fringe/overtime wage equations for one model specification and one definition of the F/W ratio are included in table A.1.

Only the latter should provide unbiased estimates. In each case, it also presents estimates of the implied annual decline in overtime hours per man and of the maximum increase in employment that would result from an increase in the overtime premium to double time.[9]

Somewhat surprisingly, the implied maximum employment effects do not vary substantially with the econometric methodology used. The Tobit estimates average 0.2 to 0.3 percentage points less than the OLS estimates on the positive overtime establishments; the latter are comparable to the results reported in table 2.5. Indeed, OLS applied to the whole sample (including zero overtime establishments) yields results similar to the Tobit results. In this sample, at least, excluding establishments with zero overtime does not significantly bias the implied employment effects.

Conclusions

What is the upper-bound estimate of the effect on employment of increasing the overtime premium to double time from time and a half? The present analyses of the 1976 *EEC* data lead to conclusions similar to those of previous investigators, who used the earlier data summarized in table 2.2. The OLS estimates of this study fall in the range of 0.5 to 1.5 percent for manufacturing and 1.0 to 2.3 percent for nonmanufacturing establishments in which overtime was initially worked (table 2.5); the 2SLS estimates are at least 2.0 to 3.0 times as large for manufacturing and 1.5 to 3.0 times as large for nonmanufacturing (table 2.6). As has been noted, however, great weight should not be placed on these findings. Finally, Tobit estimates in the nonmanufacturing sector (table 2.7), which theoretically speak-

---

9. With the linear model in equation (2.1)

OLS, whole sample	$\Delta OT = -a_1(\overline{F/W})/4$	$\%\Delta E = -(OT/20)P$
OLS, positive OT	$\Delta OT = -a_1(\overline{F/W})/4$	$\%\Delta E = -(OT/20)$
Tobit	$\Delta OT = -a_1(\overline{F/W})P/4$	$\%\Delta E = -(OT^*/20)$

ΔOT = average change in overtime hours per man
ΔOT^* = average change in overtime hours per man, taking account of changes in probability that overtime is worked
P = proportion of nonmanufacturing establishments in which overtime is worked

ing is the estimation procedure preferred to one that restricts the sample to positive overtime establishments, are only marginally lower, reducing the estimated employment gain by 0.2 to 0.3 percentage points.

These results must be qualified in a number of ways, however. First, the attempts to directly estimate the effect of a change in the overtime wage rate on overtime hours in manufacturing (from equation 2.3) met with failure; no statistically significant negative relationship was found there. The simulated employment effects reported for the manufacturing sector may be only an artifact of constraining the fringe and overtime wage coefficients to be equal and opposite sign (i.e., the employment of equation 2.2), a constraint that was rejected by formal statistical tests of the data. While this problem did not arise in the nonmanufacturing analyses, these results should reduce confidence in the belief that an increase in the overtime premium would lead to a substantial reduction in the use of overtime hours in United States manufacturing.

Second, these estimates are only maximum estimates of the number of jobs that would be created and go to currently unemployed workers. The estimates are predicated on a number of assumptions, many which may not be valid:

1. Employers' wage elasticities of demand for labor are completely inelastic; thus any reduction in overtime hours would be converted to new jobs.
2. Any reduction in the overtime hours of currently employed workers would not induce them to increase their moonlighting activities, and thus, increased moonlighting would not reduce the number of new jobs available for the unemployed.
3. Indivisibilities in production processes will not prevent any reduction in overtime hours from being converted to new full-time jobs.
4. Legislated increases in the overtime pay premium will not cause market adjustments in other conditions of employment, such as straight-time wages and fringe benefits, which will reduce employers' incentives to reduce overtime hours and increase employment.
5. The skill distributions of those working overtime and those

who are unemployed are sufficiently similar so that bottlenecks will not occur; there will always be unemployed workers available to fill the newly created positions.

6. Employers fully comply with the overtime pay provisions of the FLSA, and an increase in the overtime premium would not lead to increased noncompliance, which in turn would lead to a reduction in employers' incentives to substitute new jobs for overtime hours.

The next three chapters discuss the validity of each of these assumptions in detail and present empirical evidence on the extent to which each of the factors would constrain the job creation effects of an increase in the overtime premium.

TABLE 2.1

Coefficients of Weekly Nonwage Labor Cost
Divided by the Overtime Wage Rate Variable:
Various Studies

Industry	Ehrenberg	Solnick and Swimmer	Solnick and Swimmer	Nussbaum and Wise
Manufacturing		6.73*	17.33*	
Food	26.398*			15.68*
Textile	29.898*			14.03*
Apparel	5.137*			19.63*
Lumber	9.836			35.53*
Furniture	21.390			13.98
Paper	85.758*			42.62*
Printing	25.793*			7.59
Chemicals	25.805*			16.43*
Rubber	40.429*			9.84
Stone-clay-glass	11.029			30.08*
Primary metals	19.727*			29.53*
Fabricated metals	26.392*			23.53*
Machinery	33.695*			19.71*
Electric Equipment	32.481*			13.16*
Transportation equipment	4.121			19.00*
Instruments				−2.69
Miscellaneous manufacturing	63.146*			
Mining	0.343	0.00	47.62*	
Construction	30.959*	4.23	5.08*	
Transportation	42.888* }	−2.50	8.59	
Utilities	7.899 }			
Wholesale trade	39.093* }	11.05*	59.41*	
Retail trade	35.101* }			
Finance, insurance, and real estate	14.673	3.41	−10.05	
Services	40.370*	5.91*	41.18*	

Sources: Ehrenberg 1971a, table 3; Solnick and Swimmer 1978, table 2; Solnick and Swimmer 1978, table 3; Nussbaum and Wise 1977, table 4.3.
Note: *Coefficient statistically significantly different from zero at the 0.05 level of significance.

TABLE 2.2

Maximum Changes in Full-Time Employment
Resulting from Increasing the
Overtime Premium from Time and a Half to Double Time:
Various Studies

Study	Maximum Absolute Change	Percentage Change
Ehrenberg *1971*		
1966 manufacturing production workers	218,500	1.6%
Nussbaum and Wise *1977*		
1968 manufacturing production workers	491,400	3.7
1970 manufacturing production workers	487,700	3.7
1972 manufacturing production workers	361,900	2.8
1974 manufacturing production workers	549,700	4.0
1968–74 pooled manufacturing interindustry data employment equation estimated directly	320,000	2.0
Solnick and Swimmer *1978*		
1972 private nonfarm nonsupervisory workers (OLS analysis)	159,264	0.3
1972 private nonfarm nonsupervisory workers (3SLS analysis)	1,521,664	3.1

Sources: Ehrenberg 1971c, table 3; Nussbaum and Wise 1977, pp. 117–18 and tables 4.11, 4.11A, 4.11B, 4.11C; and Solnick and Swimmer 1978, table 5.

TABLE 2.3

Regression Coefficients of Fixed Costs
and Overtime Wage Variables:
1976 Manufacturing Data, OLS
(standard errors in parentheses)

	No Variables for Establishment-Size Code or Two-Digit SIC Code	Includes Variable for Establishment-Size Code	Includes Variables for Establishment-Size Code and Two-Digit SIC Code
$\log (F_1/W_1)$	.702 (.131)*	.673 (.135)*	.515 (.138)*
$\log (F_2/W_2)$	.500 (.107)*	.476 (.109)*	.332 (.112)*
$\log (F_3/W_3)$	.368 (.129)*	.376 (.130)*	.242 (.130)
$\log F_1$	.560 (.134)*	.548 (.136)*	.495 (.138)*
$\log W_1$	.064 (.223)	.115 (.223)	−.174 (.221)
Σ	.624 (.212)*	.663 (.215)*	.321 (.217)
$\log F_2$	.361 (.110)*	.350 (.112)*	.306 (.113)*
$\log W_2$	.284 (.212)	.327 (.211)	.015 (.212)
Σ	.645 (.200)*	.677 (.200)*	.321 (.204)
$\log F_3$	.278 (.128)*	.298 (.128)*	.241 (.130)
$\log W_3$	.419 (.202)*	.408 (.204)*	.102 (.205)
Σ	.697 (.194)*	.706 (.198)*	.343 (.204)

Notes: F_1, W_1 All fringe benefits treated as fixed costs.

F_2, W_2 Employer OASDHI contributions treated as a variable cost.

F_3, W_3 Employer OASDHI contributions and contributions to private funds (health, welfare, vacation, etc.) treated as a variable cost.

Σ Sum of log F and log W coefficients.

*Coefficient statistically significantly different from zero at the 0.05 level of significance, two-tail test.

TABLE 2.4

Regression Coefficients of Fixed Costs
and Overtime Wage Variables:
1976 Nonmanufacturing Data,
OLS on Positive Overtime Firms
(standard errors in parentheses)

	No Variables for Establishment-Size Code or Two-Digit SIC Code	Includes Variable for Establishment-Size Code	Includes Variables for Establishment-Size Code and Two-Digit SIC Code
$\log (F_1/W_1)$	1.138 (.119)*	1.154 (.119)*	1.043 (.126)*
$\log (F_2/W_2)$	0.755 (.095)*	0.780 (.095)*	0.693 (.100)*
$\log (F_3/W_3)$	0.625 (.120)*	0.621 (.121)*	0.554 (.120)*
$\log F_1$	1.129 (.122)*	1.148 (.123)*	1.049 (.127)*
$\log W_1$	-1.095 (.201)*	-1.119 (.202)*	-1.104 (.211)*
Σ	0.034 (.189)	0.029 (.191)	-0.055 (.202)
$\log F_2$	0.745 (.099)*	0.775 (.099)*	0.705 (.102)*
$\log W_2$	-0.698 (.192)*	-0.753 (.193)	-0.807 (.204)*
Σ	0.047 (.179)	0.022 (.180)	-0.102 (.192)
$\log F_3$	0.612 (.120)*	0.607 (.121)	0.562 (.120)*
$\log W_3$	-0.231 (.179)	-0.230 (.181)	-0.351 (.190)
Σ	0.381 (.176)*	0.377 (.178)*	0.211 (.192)

Notes: F_1, W_1 All fringe benefits treated as fixed costs.

$\quad\quad\ $ F_2, W_2 Employer OASDHI contributions treated as a variable cost.

$\quad\quad\ $ F_3, W_3 Employer OASDHI contributions and contributions to private funds (health, welfare, vacation, etc.) treated as a variable cost.

$\quad\quad\ $ Σ Sum of $\log F$ and $\log W$ coefficients.

$\quad\quad\ $ *Coefficient statistically significantly different from zero at the 0.05 level of significance, two-tail test.

TABLE 2.5

Implied Changes in Overtime Hours
and Employment Resulting from an
Increase in the Overtime Premium to Double Time, 1976

	Percentage Decline in Overtime			Absolute Decline in Annual Overtime Hours			Maximum Percentage Increase in Employment		
	(1)	(2)	(3)	(1)	(2)	(3)	(1)	(2)	(3)
Manufacturing[a]									
$\log(F_1/W_1)$	23.4	22.4	17.1	29.8	28.5	21.8	1.5	1.4	1.1
$\log(F_2/W_2)$	16.0	15.2	10.6	19.9	18.9	13.1	1.0	0.9	0.7
$\log(F_3/W_3)$	10.9	11.1	7.2	13.5	13.8	9.0	0.7	0.7	0.5
Nonmanufacturing[b]									
$\log(F_1/W_1)$	33.8	38.5	34.8	39.9	45.5	41.1	2.0	2.3	2.1
$\log(F_2/W_2)$	24.2	25.0	22.2	28.6	29.5	26.2	1.4	1.5	1.3
$\log(F_3/W_3)$	18.8	18.6	16.6	22.2	22.0	19.6	1.1	1.1	1.0

Notes: (1) No variables for establishment-size code or two-digit SIC code.

(2) Includes variable for establishment-size code.

(3) Includes variables for establishment-size code and two-digit SIC code.

a Based on the estimated parameters in table 2.3, evaluated at the mean values of variables in the sample.

b Based on the estimated parameters in table 2.4, evaluated at the mean values of variables in the sample. These results are for nonmanufacturing firms that initially worked their employees overtime; the sample includes 658 of the 878 nonmanufacturing establishments in the 1976 *EEC* survey.

TABLE 2.6

Regression Coefficients of
Fixed Cost-Overtime Wage
Ratio: OLS and 2SLS
(standard errors in parentheses)

	Manufacturing		Nonmanfacturing	
	OLS	2SLS	OLS	2SLS
No ESC				
$\log (F_1/W_1)$	0.702 (.131)	1.760 (.317)	1.138 (.119)	1.632 (.289)
$\log (F_2/W_2)$	0.500 (.107)	1.417 (.253)	0.755 (.095)	1.024 (.220)
$\log (F_3/W_3)$	0.368 (.129)	1.811 (.419)	0.625 (.120)	1.633 (.546)
ESC included				
$\log (F_1/W_1)$	0.673 (.135)	2.116 (.405)	1.154 (.119)	1.772 (.301)
$\log (F_2/W_2)$	0.476 (.109)	1.659 (.311)	0.780 (.095)	1.179 (.228)
$\log (F_3/W_3)$	0.376 (.130)	2.265 (.492)	0.621 (.121)	1.815 (.630)

Note: ESC Establishment-size code variables.

TABLE 2.7

Increasing Overtime Premium to Double Time
in Nonmanufacturing Industry: Tobit Results
(absolute *t*-statistics in parentheses)

	Coefficient	Absolute Decline in Annual Overtime/Man	Maximum Percentage Increase in Employment
No Intercept Shift			
OLS: whole sample	18.498 (9.0)	29.63	1.2%
OLS: positive overtime establishment	18.037 (8.0)	28.90	1.4
Tobit	20.690 (8.6)	28.46	1.2
Establishment-size Intercept Shifts			
OLS: whole sample	18.856 (9.0)	30.21	1.3
OLS: positive overtime establishment	18.895 (8.3)	30.27	1.5
Tobit	20.739 (8.6)	28.55	1.2
Establishment-size and Industry Intercept Shifts			
OLS: whole sample	16.272 (7.2)	26.07	1.1
OLS: positive overtime establishment	15.882 (6.4)	25.44	1.3
Tobit	17.884 (6.9)	24.70	1.0

Note: Sample sizes are 878 for Tobit and whole sample and 658 for positive overtime regressions.

3 · CONSTRAINTS ON THE EMPLOYMENT EFFECTS OF AN INCREASE IN THE OVERTIME PREMIUM

Nonzero Wage Elasticities

The estimates presented in the previous chapter assume that the demand for man-hours is completely inelastic. That is, they ignore the fact that an increase in the overtime premium raises the average cost per man-hour of labor; this may induce a shift to more capital-intensive methods of production and, to the extent that the cost increase is passed on to consumers in the form of higher prices, a reduction in the quantity of output demanded. Both the substitution and scale effects should lead to a decline in the number of man-hours used by employers.

It is possible to make a crude estimate of the magnitude of these effects. Daniel Hamermesh (1976) has surveyed time-series estimates of the wage elasticity of demand for labor and has concluded that a reasonable estimate for the long-run (four-quarter) elasticity is −0.3 (it should be noted that virtually all the studies he cited used man-hours as the measure of labor and failed to include nonwage labor costs in their analyses). Suppose that before an increase in the overtime premium the standard workweek was 40 hours and employees averaged 3 hours of overtime per week. Suppose also that the increase in the overtime premium induced a reduction of 1.2 hours of overtime per week; the latter figure would lead to a 3 percent increase in full-time employment *if* total man-hours remained constant and the new employees did not work any overtime. Now the reduction in overtime coupled with the increase in the premium to double time would cause the average hourly wage rate which includes overtime payments, to rise by about 0.8 percent.[1] This would imply a 0.24 percent decline in total man-hours and an increase in employment of roughly 2.75 percent. Thus, the estimate of the maximum number of new jobs created would fall by about 0.25 percentage points once the existence of nonzero wage elasticities of demand is accounted for.[2]

Moonlighting

Would any new jobs that resulted from an increase in the overtime premium actually go to individuals who were unemployed? The previous chapter's estimates also neglect supply-side responses of currently employed workers, who would simultaneously face an increase in the overtime premium and a reduction in their hours of work. One possible response is increased moonlighting at part-time jobs; this would further constrain the creation of new jobs for the unemployed.

Previous investigators have discounted the possibility that increased moonlighting would hinder employment creation (U.S., Department of Labor 1967). Among the evidence they cite are the facts that very little moonlighting occurs in the economy (less than 5 percent of all employed workers had second jobs in 1978), that many moonlighters' primary jobs are in agriculture, and that moonlighters tend to be employed in lower skill-level positions than their primary jobs, which reduces the attractiveness of moonlighting as a substitute for overtime (see Rosenfeld 1979 and Brown 1978 for data on multiple job-holding and Perloff and Wachter 1978 for analyses of the likely effects of moonlighting on work-sharing arrangements).

---

1. The percentage wage gain is given by $((40W + (2.0)(1.8)W)/41.8)/ ((40W + (1.5)(3.0)W)/43)$.

2. There is a certain inconsistency in the procedure used here. It clearly would be preferable to estimate hours per man and employment level equations together as part of a simultaneous system and then to derive the estimated employment effects directly from this system. Unfortunately, no micro level (individual establishment) data set is available that permits this.

The small number of individuals currently holding second jobs, however, is not indicative of the potential expansion in moonlighting that might occur if overtime hours were severely restricted. Between 1973 and 1978, roughly 27 percent of all wage and salary workers who had only one job regularly worked more than forty hours a week (Stamas 1979). If overtime were restricted, many of these individuals might seek second jobs. Clearly, evidence on the relationship between overtime hours and moonlighting is required.

Two recent studies have dealt with the effect of weekly hours of work on the moonlighting decision, Shishko and Rostker (1976) and Connell (1979); the former uses data from the Michigan Income Dynamics Panel Study, the latter data from the National Longitudinal Survey.[3] It was possible, based upon Shishko and Rostker, to perform simulations of the effects of a simultaneous reduction in overtime hours and increase in the overtime premium both on the probability that an individual moonlights and on his or her average hours on the second job if moonlighting does occur. These analyses suggest that a simultaneous reduction in overtime hours of two hours per week and an increase in the overtime premium to double time would lead to an increase of about 6 percent in moonlighting hours (for details of these calculations, see Appendix B). Given the currently low level of moonlighting, this crude calculation suggests that it is unlikely that increased moonlighting would be a substantial deterrent to the employment creation effects of an increase in the overtime premium.

-----

3. Neither of the studies cited is completely satisfactory. They both assume that overtime hours of work on individuals' primary jobs are solely employer determined and that individuals do not have the right to refuse overtime. In fact, data from the *1977 Quality of Employment Survey,* conducted by the Michigan Survey Research Center for the U.S. Department of Labor, indicate that 44 percent of the workers in the sample who regularly worked overtime reported that it was "mostly up to the worker whether he or she works overtime," and another 29 percent reported that it was "mostly up to the employer, but that the worker can refuse without penalty." Indeed, only for 16 percent was the decision solely up to the employer and could the worker not refuse overtime without a penalty (Quinn and Staines 1977, pp. 90–91). While these data may overstate the freedom that individual workers actually have in choosing overtime hours, they do suggest that the overtime hour–moonlighting relationship is much more complicated than the models used in previous research imply.

Indivisibilities

The maximum employment gain estimates ignore two types of indivisibilities. First, there are indivisibilities associated with an integrated team production process. Specialization and division of labor within an enterprise may give rise to time complementarities among workers and between workers and capital that may prevent the substitution of additional employment for hours (Rosen 1978). For example, a firm in a continuous process industry may regularly use its existing work force an average of two hours a week overtime by scheduling shifts of 40, 40, 40, and 48 hours (24 × 7 = 168 hours). If men-machine ratios are relatively fixed, at least in the short run, it would be difficult to substitute new, full-time employment for hours in such a firm.

Second, there are indivisibilities associated with establishment size. While a large establishment may have the option of substituting one new full-time employee for the overtime hours of twenty employees who each work two hours a week overtime, small establishments with only a few employees working overtime may not enjoy such options. Following this line of reasoning, an increase in the overtime premium might induce a substitution of additional employment for overtime hours in large establishments, while indivisibilities might prevent such substitutions from occurring in smaller establishments and result in those establishments being placed at a relative cost disadvantage. If this were the likely outcome, policy makers might contemplate having any increase in the overtime premium apply only to establishments above a minimum size; historically there have been size-class exemptions under various provisions of the FLSA for similar reasons.[4] Reducing the number of firms required to pay an increase in the premium would reduce the estimated employment gain associated with the increase.

A previous study has attempted to ascertain if the relationship between the use of overtime hours and the ratio of quasi-fixed nonwage cost to overtime wage rate does vary across size classes of

---

4. Exemptions for reasons of establishment size have declined over time. The 1978 amendment to the FLSA, however, did increase the annual sales level that retail trade establishments had to exceed before they became subject to the overtime provisions.

establishments (Ehrenberg 1971a, chaps. 5 and 6). For the non-manufacturing industries, Ehrenberg found that the relationship was fairly stable across all size classes of establishments within each major nonmanufacturing industry; small establishments appeared to alter their relative usage of employment and hours in response to a change in the ratio in a similar manner to large establishments.[5] The results for the manufacturing sector were quite different, however. For these industries, the marginal effect of an increase in the overtime premium on hours did vary across size classes of establishments within each two-digit industry. There was, however, no consistent pattern across industries in the way the magnitude and the statistical significance of the effect varied with establishment size. Indeed, in several cases, it was the smallest size classes of establishments for which the largest marginal effects were observed. Since the magnitude and statistical significance of the relationship between the use of overtime hours and the ratio of the quasi-fixed nonwage cost to the overtime wage rate does not appear to vary across size classes of establishments in any systematic way across manufacturing industries, it would not appear reasonable to institute a set of size class exemptions for any increase in the overtime premium.[6]

Compensating Wage and Fringe Benefit Adjustments

An additional shortcoming of the employment gain simulations reported in Chapter 2 is that they ignore the possibility that an increase in the overtime premium may lead to compensating adjustments in straight-time wages, fringe benefits, or both. For example, suppose that firms and their employees are initially in an equilib-

---

5. In that study, establishments were grouped into eight size classes; less than 20 employees, 20 to 49, 50 to 99, 100 to 249, 250 to 499, 500 to 999, 1,000 to 2,499, and 2,500 or more employees.

6. It is possible that the sample sizes used in the manufacturing industry analyses reported in Ehrenberg 1971 were too small (an average of 60 establishments per two-digit industry as compared to an average of 150 in each nonmanufacturing industry) to precisely estimate how the effects varied with establishment size. Unfortunately, the sample size in the *EEC* data has been reduced over time (from over 4,000 manufacturing establishments in 1966 to less than 2,000 manufacturing and nonmanufacturing establishments in 1976) so that it may never prove possible to resolve this issue.

rium situation in which overtime hours are regularly scheduled. From employers' perspectives, one plausible response to a legislated increase in the overtime premium is for them to attempt to reduce the level, or rate of growth, of straight-time wages and fringes. If they are successful, and the total compensation of workers for the initial equilibrium level of hours, including overtime, remains the same as it would have been in the absence of the legislated change, one may argue that employers would have no incentive to reduce their usage of overtime hours.

Actually, this argument is a bit simplistic. From the employer's perspective what is relevant in the determination of overtime hours is not the overall level of labor costs but rather the ratio R of quasi-fixed weekly labor costs per employee F to the overtime wage rate W; the latter is the product of the straight-time wage S and the overtime premium P

$$R = F/SP. \tag{3.1}$$

The simulations reported in the previous chapter assume that an increase in P induces no change in either S or F. What is certainly true is that *if* a compensating decline in straight-time wages occurs, the decline in R will be smaller and the resulting decrease in hours and increase in employment smaller in absolute value than the simulations reported. As equation 3.1 indicates, however, a compensating decline in the quasi-fixed costs F would cause the actual decline in R to be larger and the resulting decrease in hours and increase in employment would be larger in absolute value than the simulations indicate, ceteris paribus. As such, one cannot predict a priori what the direction of the bias is here; it depends upon the extent, if any, to which compensating adjustments occur in both straight-time wages and fringes.

Evidence on the magnitudes, if any, of these compensating adjustments is required before it can be concluded that their omission substantially biases the estimated employment gains that would result from increasing the overtime premium. As part of this study, attempts were made to use the 1976 *EEC* data to test whether an inverse relationship exists across establishments between straight-time wages or fringe benefits or both and the magnitude of the overtime premium, ceteris paribus. Unfortunately, a simultaneous equations model of the determinants of wages, fringe benefits, and the overtime premium that enabled the identification of whether such trade-offs exist could not be constructed. One of the reasons for this is that cross-section variations in the overtime premium are due both to collective bargaining agreements and differences in coverage under the FLSA, making it difficult to disentangle the effects of legislated and collectively bargained differences in the premium. This remains, then, an area in which further research is needed.[7]

---

7. It is somewhat paradoxical that for years researchers have analyzed the employment effects of minimum wage changes without considering the possibility that there might be *none* because firms can potentially respond to an increase in the minimum by reducing nonwage forms of compensation for low-wage workers. Of course, one might argue that due to the limitation on the total compensation that low-skill labor would receive, even in the absence of the minimum, that there is no room for an increase in the minimum to reduce other forms of compensation (i.e., they are close to zero already). Nevertheless, this too remains an empirical issue. See Wessels 1980 for a more detailed discussion of this point.

4 · THE SKILL DISTRIBUTIONS OF THE UNEMPLOYED AND THOSE WHO WORK OVERTIME

Initial Comparisons

If an increase in the overtime premium led to a substantial reduction in the usage of overtime hours, would this reduction be converted to new full-time jobs that would go to the unemployed? In part the answer depends upon whether the skill distributions of the unemployed and those who work overtime are sufficiently similar to permit the substitution of jobs for overtime hours.

Data are available in the annual May *Current Population Survey (CPS)* on the occupational distribution of both the experienced unemployed and those who work overtime for premium pay. Table 4.1 presents tabulations made from the May 1978 *CPS* tapes for major (one-digit) occupational groups at the national level. The first column records the total number of individuals working overtime for premium pay during the survey week, and the second column the total number of overtime hours worked for premium pay during the week. If one assumes that 20 percent of these overtime hours would be eliminated and converted to new, full-time jobs because of an increase in the premium to double time, a percentage in line with the estimates presented in Chapter 2, it is possible to compute the number of new jobs that potentially might be created; these calculations appear in the third column. Finally, the fourth column tabulates the number of experienced unemployed in each occupational group.

At first glance these estimates suggest that skill mismatches are unlikely to constrain the substitution of new employees for overtime hours. A 20 percent reduction in overtime hours in this sample would lead to a maximum of 350,000 newly created jobs; at the same time, the experienced unemployed totaled some 4,828,000 individuals. Indeed, only for craftsmen and kindred is the ratio of the experienced unemployed to the potential number of newly created jobs as low as five to one.

One should not place too much faith, however, in conclusions drawn from the data in table 4.1. The use of aggregate one-digit occupational data may obscure more than it reveals. The range of narrow occupational categories within each broad category is vast; for example, the craftsmen category includes bakers, carpenters, tailors, and stationary engineers. To draw any meaningful conclusions about potential skill-mix bottlenecks requires that analyses be conducted at a more detailed occupational level. Moreover, the relevant geographic level to conduct analyses at is the local labor market level. Until such analyses are undertaken, no firm conclusions can be drawn; therefore, similar estimates for more detailed occupational and geographic breakdowns follow.

Table 4.2 presents data on the distributions of the experienced unemployed and the estimated number of new jobs that would be created if 20 percent of the overtime hours worked for premium pay were converted to new full-time jobs, cross-tabulated by major occupational groups and the nine census geographic divisions. Again, these estimates do not suggest widespread skill mismatches. The only cell with a sizable number of cases in which the number of experienced unemployed individuals is less than the potential number of newly created jobs induced by an increase in the premium is the one for transportation equipment operatives in the west north central region; and in this case it is an excess of only 1,100 jobs (2,900 − 1,800). Moreover, the ratio of the experienced unemployed to the potential number of new jobs is over two to one in all but one of the cells for craftsmen and operatives, the occupations in which over half the new jobs would be created.

Detailed Comparisons

Although table 4.2 makes regional comparisons, it still considers only the broad occupational categories. Table 4.3 considers the detailed census three-digit occupational categories at the national level. The columns in this table are identical to those in table 4.1, save that the statistics are now in hundreds rather than thousands. At this level of detail, skill mismatches begin to become evident, even when the analyses are conducted at the national level. The occupations in which the potential number of jobs created would exceed the number of experienced unemployed are indicated by an asterisk. Considering all these occupations in which the potential number of jobs created exceeds the number of experienced unemployed, a total of 19,400 potential new jobs, or 5.5 percent of the 350,000 total estimated in table 4.1, might go unfilled because there would not be experienced unemployed individuals available to fill them. The largest number of unfilled jobs, some 4,000, would occur in the telephone installer and repairman category.

These calculations may severely underestimate the constraints on new job creation because they are done on the national level and ignore local area or regional imbalances, an issue that will be addressed shortly. On the other hand, this estimate assumes that only an unemployed individual who has previous experience in an occupation can fill job vacancies in the occupation. For some unskilled jobs, e.g., the various skilled trade apprentice categories, this is clearly an unrealistic assumption. Moreover, for other occupations it may be reasonable to assume that employers can easily train inexperienced unemployed individuals for the positions or can upgrade existing lower skilled workers and then fill their positions with the unemployed. The issue ultimately may not be whether a sufficient number of experienced unemployed individuals exist to fill these potentials jobs, but rather whether the time and money costs of training new employees will limit job creation. Clearly, tabulations such as those in table 4.3 cannot answer this question.

While it might be desirable to conduct similar analyses at the three-digit occupational level by geographical region, the size of the resulting table if all the three-digit occupations were included would overwhelm any reader. Moreover, as noted above, in some cases the three-digit level may well be too narrow for these purposes; an unemployed individual may be employable in a number of different three-digit occupations. To focus on both regional and occupational imbalances simultaneously, the next table therefore restricts itself to the categories for craftsmen and operative, the ones in which table 4.1 suggests more than half the jobs would be created, and contrast the potential number of new jobs created to the number of experienced unemployed for thirteen separate occupational categories, many much broader than the three-digit level, in each of the nine geographic divisions. These thirteen occupational categories, in fact, encompass all the craftsmen and operatives in the sample.

Table 4.4 does suggest regional imbalances exist, even at the broader occupational category level considered here. A box calls out each occupation in the table for which the number of experienced unemployed is less than the potential number of new jobs created by the increase in the overtime premium. For example, while the number of experienced unemployed in the category of foremen substantially exceeds the potential number of new jobs created in the Middle Atlantic states, the reverse occurs in the New England states and the East and West North Central states. Unless unemployed individuals are willing to move across these broad geographic regions, skill mismatches may well limit new job creation. To get an idea of the magnitude of the problem, one may add up the differences between the potential number of new jobs created and the number of the experienced unemployed, across all occupation-region cells in table 4.4 in which this difference is positive. The sum turns out to be 15,500, or approximately 8.5 percent of the 182,000 jobs that table 4.1 indicates would potentially be created in the craftsmen and operatives categories.

Finally, table 4.5 performs similar calculations for twenty-one selected detailed three-digit craftsmen and operative categories by geographic division. These categories were chosen because they represent the occupations in which a substantial number of the potential newly created jobs would occur, at least 2,000 nationwide in each category and some 120,027 in total. In addition, these occupational categories all require considerable job-specific skills; if experienced unemployed individuals were not available, employers could not fill any job vacancies without making substantial investments in training.

These calculations suggest that skill mismatches of the distributions of those working overtime and the experienced unemployed may well seriously constrain the creation of new jobs in response to an increase in the overtime premium in these categories. There are many detailed occupation-geographic cells in this table in which the number of experienced unemployed is less than the potential number of new jobs created. Moreover, the excess of the potential number of jobs created over the experienced unemployed, across those occupation-geographic division cells in which the excess is positive, totals 28,103. This is over 23 percent of the total number of potential new jobs created in these categories. Indeed, even if there were *no* skill mismatches in any other geographic division–occupation cells, a highly dubious assumption given the results in tables 4.1 through 4.4, the estimated potential overall employment gain of 350,000 would fall by some 8.5 percent.

Summary of Results

Are the skill distributions of the unemployed and those who work overtime sufficiently dissimilar to severely limit the number of new jobs that would be created in response to an increase in the overtime premium that reduced the number of overtime hours by 20 percent? The analyses presented here suggest that they are. Focusing on either national (table 4.1) or regional (table 4.2) data at the one-digit census occupational level yields no evidence of skill mismatches. Analyses at the three-digit occupational level that ignored regional imbalances (table 4.3), however, suggest that 5.5 percent of the potential number of jobs created could not be filled. Moreover, when regional imbalances are considered as well, this figure rises to 8.5 percent of the craftsmen and operative jobs, even when rather broad occupational categories (table 4.4) are used. Furthermore, when one focuses on regional imbalances and twenty-one detailed three-digit census craftsmen and operative categories—occupations in which over one-third of the potential new jobs would be created and occupations that require highly skilled workers—one finds that skill mismatches would prevent over 23 percent of the job creation. Indeed, these mismatches alone would reduce the estimated overall employment gain for all occupations by some 8.5 percent.

It is, of course, important to note the limitations of these calculations. First, these calculations ignore the fact that the *CPS* is not a complete census; as a result standard errors should really be attached to all the numbers in the tables. This might cause some numbers that appear different from each other to actually fail to be judged statistically significantly so. To derive standard errors, however, would not be a trivial task.

Second, these estimates assume that there would be no mobility of unemployed individuals across the nine census divisions in response to increase job opportunities in other areas. While such mobility would cause the estimates presented here to overstate the extent of skill mismatches, it should be also be pointed out that the estimates implicitly assumed perfect mobility within a census division. So, for example, if there were a vacancy for a carpenter in New York City and an unemployed carpenter lived some 350 miles away in Buffalo, these calculations assume that a job match would be made. Such an assumption is overoptimistic, to say the least, and it causes the estimates to also understate the extent of skill mismatches.[1]

Third, in places these estimates assume that only an unemployed individual with previous work experience in a three-digit occupation can fill the new jobs created in the occupation. For some unskilled jobs this is clearly an unrealistic assumption. For other more skilled occupations, such as those listed in table 4.5, the question is really whether employers will be willing to make the investments of money and time necessary to train unemployed individuals or to upgrade existing unskilled employees to fill potential vacancies. A quick perusal of table 4.5 suggests, however, that in the main these are occupations with high training costs, and many are located in the building trades where union rules restrict entry. Hence, it is not evident that an increase in the overtime premium would induce employers to train more individuals for these jobs.

Fourth, these estimates ignore the possibility that employers

---

1. Further analyses of regional imbalances could be done at the individual state level with the *CPS* data. The sample sizes for many states, however, would be extremely small, which would limit the usefulness of the analyses.

would substitute additional employment of unemployed unskilled workers for overtime hours of skilled workers. Since an increase in the overtime premium would increase the average hourly (including overtime) cost of skilled workers relative to the average hourly cost of unskilled workers not working overtime such substitution might occur. The available evidence does tend to indicate that different skill groups are substitutes in production; however, the estimates of cross-wage elasticities of demand are not precise enough to evaluate how this would affect the results (Hamermesh and Grant 1979).

Finally, these estimates refer to a single point in time, May 1978. In periods when unemployment is higher and the use of overtime lower, skill bottlenecks are less likely to constrain job creation. Conversely, in periods of lower unemployment and greater use of overtime, skill bottlenecks are likely to be more important.

TABLE 4.1

Experienced Unemployed, Overtime Hours, and
Estimated Number of Jobs Created by
Conversion of 20 Percent of the Overtime,
by Major Occupational Groups (× 1,000)

Occupation	Number Working Overtime for Premium Pay	Overtime Hours for Premium Pay per Week	New Full-time Jobs Created	Experienced Unemployed
Professional, technical and kindred	546	5,172	26	324
Managers and administrators	318	3,315	17	197
Sales workers	145	1,323	7	260
Clerical and kindred	984	6,976	35	870
Craftsmen and kindred	1,952	19,842	99	493
Operatives, except transport	1,780	16,503	83	949
Transport equipment operatives	565	6,691	33	202
Nonfarm laborers	476	4,959	25	468
Private household workers	2	9	0[a]	57
All other service workers	421	4,525	23	924
Farmers and farm managers	2	35	0[a]	2
Farm laborers and foremen	23	484	2	82
Total	7,214	69,834	350	4,828

Source: Author's calculations from U.S., Department of Commerce, Bureau of the Census 1978.
Cited in table sources hereinafter as May 1978 *CPS*.

Note: 0 denotes less than 500.

TABLE 4.2

Experienced Unemployed and
Estimated Number of New Jobs Created by
Conversion of 20 Percent of Hours Worked for Premium Pay,
by Major Occupational Group and Geographic Division ($\times$ 100)

Occupation	New England	Middle Atlantic	East North Central	West North Central	South Atlantic	East South Central	West South Central	Mountain	Pacific
Professional, technical, and kindred									
Unemployed	242	846	427	259	385	187	82	135	673
Jobs created	12	39	69	18	27	12	43	15	24
Managers and administrators									
Unemployed	239	362	288	84	287	87	193	56	377
Jobs created	5	20	33	14	31	4	28	10	22
Sales workers									
Unemployed	119	536	598	185	326	96	167	133	434
Jobs created	11	10	8	7	5	5	12	10	7
Clerical and kindred									
Unemployed	456	1,905	1,572	334	1,454	410	689	369	1,509
Jobs created	18	35	79	31	58	16	45	14	52
Craftsmen and kindred									
Unemployed	234	1,249	850	177	598	276	250	194	1,101
Jobs created	56	111	259	62	157	67	130	45	104
Operatives, except transport									
Unemployed	448	1,963	1,773	401	1,465	774	744	285	1,630
Jobs created	55	86	233	49	117	68	102	32	82

TABLE 4.2 (*continued*)

Occupation	New England	Middle Atlantic	East North Central	West North Central	South Atlantic	East South Central	West South Central	Mountain	Pacific
Transport equipment operatives									
Unemployed	81	526	593	18	242	43	78	114	321
Jobs created	17	35	77	29	40	25	44	22	44
Nonfarm laborers									
Unemployed	293	883	938	237	759	319	284	199	764
Jobs created	10	24	71	27	24	17	35	12	28
Private household workers									
Unemployed	80	78	96	50	67	28	65	30	80
Jobs created	0	0	0	0	0	0	0	0	0
All other service workers									
Unemployed	455	1,516	1,970	526	1,508	508	737	584	1,432
Jobs created	14	32	41	21	41	10	17	9	4
Farmers and farm managers									
Unemployed	0	0	0	0	0	0	20	4	0
Jobs created	0	0	1	0	0	0	0	1	0
Farm laborers and foremen									
Unemployed	6	100	112	44	75	31	159	26	266
Jobs created	0	0	4	8	1	0	2	0	10

Source: Author's calculations from the May 1978 *CPS*.
Note: 0 denotes fewer than 50.

TABLE 4.3

Experienced Unemployed,
Overtime Hours Worked for Premium Pay,
and Estimated Number of New Jobs Created by
Conversion of 20 Percent of Overtime,
by Detailed Occupational Group (× 100)

Occupation	Number Working Overtime for Premium Pay	Overtime Hours Worked for Premium Pay/Week	New Full-time Jobs Created	Experienced Unemployed
Professional, technical, and kindred				
Accountants	330	2,543	13	250
*Architects	17	345	2	0
Computer programmers	26	212	1	24
Computer systems analysts	54	353	2	19
*Aeronautical engineers	78	1,125	6	0
Civil engineers	46	386	2	54
*Electrical engineers	198	2,464	12	0
Industrial engineers	98	1,320	7	48
*Mechanical engineers	217	1,961	10	0
*Mining engineers	16	128	1	0
Sales engineers	10	48	0	0
Engineers (n.e.c.)	114	876	4	55
Foresters	77	696	3	34
Statisticians	14	14	0	17
Agricultural scientists	5	30	0	0
Biological scientists	21	42	0	0
*Chemists	18	143	1	0
Geologists	20	95	0	0
*Physicists	19	379	2	0
Life scientists (n.e.c.)	16	158	1	0
Operations researchers	51	324	2	18
Labor relations workers	68	484	2	117
Pharmacists	96	521	3	6
Physicians	19	188	1	17
Registered nurses	911	5,388	27	168
Therapists	62	397	2	73
Lab technicians	134	1,396	7	39
Health technicians	16	81	0	0
Radiology technicians	5	50	0	35
Health technicians (n.e.c.)	62	1,032	5	102
Clergymen	12	542	2	51
Economists	36	362	2	18
Psychologists	18	55	0	0
Social workers	90	1,346	7	121
Recreation workers	27	213	1	172
Business teachers	15	30	0	0
Adult education teachers	13	66	0	32
Elementary school teachers	31	209	1	179
Nursery teachers	16	129	1	107
Secondary school teachers	69	399	2	106
Other noncollege teachers	49	2,008	10	40
Agricultural technicians	60	908	5	32
Chemical technicians	53	562	3	42
Draftsmen	436	3,475	17	59

TABLE 4.3 (continued)

Occupation	Number Working Overtime for Premium Pay	Overtime Hours Worked for Premium Pay/Week	New Full-time Jobs Created	Experienced Unemployed
Electrical technicians	543	6,841	34	16
Industrial technicians	17	174	1	15
*Mechanical eng. technicians	23	180	1	0
Surveyors	207	1,979	10	24
Eng. technicians (n.e.c.)	437	4,697	23	42
Airplane pilots	20	120	1	2
Radio operators	82	726	4	58
Technicians (n.e.c.)	4	80	0	0
Vocational counselors	9	47	0	78
Athletes	15	153	1	34
Designers	86	484	2	70
Editors and reporters	27	292	1	134
Musicians and composers	33	326	2	116
*Painters and sculptors	76	1,046	5	1
Photographers	57	759	4	29
Public relations	19	117	1	70
Radio and TV announcers	3	6	0	0
Writers and artists (n.e.c.)	32	119	1	51
Research workers (n.e.c.)	18	92	0	68
Managers and administrators, except farm				
*Bank officers and managers	105	1,385	7	0
Buyers and shippers, farm products	17	171	1	0
*Buyers, wholesale & retail	23	160	1	30
Credit men	43	171	1	14
Health administrators	21	146	1	50
Construction inspectors	18	92	0	10
Other inspectors	115	1,314	7	15
Office managers (n.e.c.)	97	781	4	77
*Officers on ships	70	1,316	7	0
Public administrators	135	1,321	7	47
Union officials	16	156	1	19
Purchasing agents	132	1,265	6	83
*Railroad conductors	77	980	5	0
Food service managers	188	1,820	9	260
Managers, retail trade	342	2,487	12	115
Managers, other	69	542	3	23
Managers (n.e.c.)	1,711	19,045	95	1,082
Sales workers				
Advertising agents	37	197	1	5
Insurance agents	67	481	2	105
Newsboys	16	16	0	10
Sales reps., manuf.	126	921	5	85
Sales reps., wholesale tr.	236	2,977	14	164
Sales clerks, retail tr.	695	6,866	34	1,628

TABLE 4.3 (*continued*)

Occupation	Number Working Overtime for Premium Pay	Overtime Hours Worked for Premium Pay/Week	New Full-time Jobs Created	Experienced Unemployed
Salesmen, retail tr.	205	1,562	8	269
Other salesmen	65	308	2	178
Clerical and kindred				
Bank tellers	267	1,337	7	104
Building clerks	92	747	4	21
Bookkeepers	745	4,528	23	499
Cashiers	589	4,391	22	1,324
Clerical supervisors	92	601	3	77
Bill collectors	23	175	2	20
Counter clerks, nonfood	294	1,986	10	242
*Vehicle dispatchers	200	2,237	11	0
Enumerators	16	32	0	81
Estimators (n.e.c.)	234	1,289	6	172
Product controllers	411	3,493	17	27
File clerks	125	814	4	391
Insurance adjustors	54	342	2	40
Library attendents	20	117	1	67
Mail carriers, post office	508	2,998	15	47
Mail handlers, other	55	521	3	137
Calculating machine operators	39	678	3	16
Computer operators	565	5,694	28	202
Key punch operators	187	1,262	6	144
Office machine operators	32	199	1	95
Payroll clerks	356	2,745	14	760
Postal clerks	363	2,375	12	67
Proofreaders	84	587	3	9
Receptionists	185	832	4	324
Secretaries, legal	6	29	0	85
Secretaries, medical	34	205	1	30
Secretaries (n.e.c.)	919	4,534	22	1,147
Shipping clerks	830	6,879	34	378
Statistical clerks	243	1,843	9	108
Stenographers	17	349	2	14
Stock clerks	618	4,783	23	352
*Telegraph operators	36	536	3	0
Telephone operators	200	842	4	238
Ticket agents	106	650	3	33
Typists	313	1,988	10	828
Weighers	55	337	2	34
Misc. clerical workers	781	5,961	30	681
Clerical workers (n.e.c.)	143	849	4	252
Craftsmen and kindred				
Automobile installers	17	203	1	17
Bakers	36	185	1	81
Boilermakers	120	1,693	8	41
Bookbinders	68	369	2	34

TABLE 4.3 (*continued*)

Occupation	Number Working Overtime for Premium Pay	Overtime Hours Worked for Premium Pay/Week	New Full-time Jobs Created	Experienced Unemployed
Brickmasons	72	1,211	6	130
Bulldozer operator	155	2,074	10	25
*Cabinet makers	35	378	2	0
Carpenters	892	8,675	43	652
Carpet installers	72	538	3	57
Cement masons	107	1,294	6	51
Typesetters	277	1,820	9	57
Cranemen et al.	490	5,401	27	60
Decorators	73	886	4	53
Electricians	1,091	13,311	67	181
*Electricians apprent.	88	831	4	0
*Electric power lineman	206	2,304	12	0
*Engravers	29	244	1	0
Excavating machine oper.	629	6,355	32	122
Floor layers	19	96	0	0
Foremen (n.e.c.)	2,697	28,968	145	371
*Forgemen	12	107	1	0
*Furniture finishers	32	319	2	0
Glaziers	7	29	0	23
Heat treaters	48	316	2	23
Inspectors	36	495	2	2
Inspectors (n.e.c.)	85	597	3	16
Job and die setters	292	3,310	17	39
Locomotive engineers	133	1,371	7	18
*Machinists	1,385	14,068	70	191
Machinists, apprent.	80	792	4	0
*Mechanics, appliance	361	3,824	19	169
Mechanics, aircraft	152	1,805	9	0
Mechanics, auto body	86	418	2	45
Mechanics, auto	1,385	12,930	65	251
Data processing machine repairmen	217	1,455	7	18
*Mechanics, farm impl.	127	1,573	8	0
*Mechanics, heavy equip.	2,552	26,722	134	169
Mechanics, household appl.	235	1,543	8	21
Loom fixers	23	184	1	0
Office machine, mech.	97	728	4	6
Radio & T.V. mech.	62	499	2	14
Railroad and car, mech.	45	495	2	5
Mechanic, apprent.	14	14	0	0
Misc., mech.	366	4,440	22	76
*Mech. (n.e.c.)	44	763	4	0
*Millers	24	340	2	0
Millwrights	239	2,061	10	57
Molders, metal	17	314	2	15
Opticians	17	83	0	41
Painters	248	1882	9	533
*Pattern makers	105	911	5	0

TABLE 4.3 (*continued*)

Occupation	Number Working Overtime for Premium Pay	Overtime Hours Worked for Premium Pay/Week	New Full-time Jobs Created	Experienced Unemployed
Photo engravers	80	531	3	37
Plasterers	19	151	1	94
Plumbers	671	6,596	33	358
*Plumbers, apprent.	18	156	1	0
*Power station oper.	56	481	2	0
Pressmen	242	2,272	11	51
*Pressmen, apprent.	42	298	1	0
*Rollers and finishers	91	652	3	0
Roofers and slaters	51	518	3	143
Sheetmetal workers	237	2,194	11	88
*Sheetmetal apprent.	75	601	3	0
Shoe repairman	11	28	0	14
*Sign painters	6	121	1	0
Stationery engineers	251	2,558	13	31
Structural metal craftsmen	52	516	3	43
*Telephone installers & rep.	692	8,007	40	0
Telephone linemen	186	1,576	8	33
Tile setters	17	86	0	35
Tool and die, makers	740	7,493	37	74
*Tool and die, apprent.	33	328	2	0
Upholsterers	19	56	0	19
Apprentices (n.e.c.)	50	419	2	19
*Apprentices (n.e.c.)	53	477	2	0
Craftsmen (n.e.c.)	128	1,005	5	103
Operatives, except transport				
Asbestos workers	73	963	5	99
Assemblers	1,888	15,244	76	941
*Blasters	43	526	3	0
Bottling operatives	90	561	3	49
*Chainmen	29	187	1	0
Checkers	1,539	13,012	65	564
Clothing ironers	50	213	1	138
Cutting operatives	447	4,197	21	207
Dressmakers	9	27	0	118
Drillers	127	1,767	9	58
Dry wall installers	21	379	2	110
Dyers	49	315	2	42
Filers	243	1,817	9	33
Furnacemen	78	683	3	50
Garage workers	311	3,308	17	474
Graders and sorters	32	194	1	163
Produce packers	18	109	0	0
Metal heaters	18	144	0	0
Laundry operatives	148	2,467	12	144
Meat cutters, nonman.	433	3,355	17	102
Meat cutters, man.	193	1,221	6	126
Meat wrappers	43	172	1	17

TABLE 4.3 (*continued*)

Occupation	Number Working Overtime for Premium Pay	Overtime Hours Worked for Premium Pay/Week	New Full-time Jobs Created	Experienced Unemployed
Metal platters	115	1,371	7	34
Mine operatives (n.e.c.)	484	8,580	43	120
Mixing operatives	230	3,603	18	52
Oilers and greasers	134	2,244	11	50
Packers and wrappers	713	5,552	28	912
Painters	322	2,424	12	208
Photographic workers	83	460	2	53
Drill press oper.	121	996	5	17
Grinding mach. oper.	396	4,143	21	133
Lathe operators	356	3,360	17	70
Operators (n.e.c.)	192	1,693	8	136
Punch press oper.	447	4,415	22	98
Riveters	71	427	2	44
Sailors	69	2,922	15	54
Sawyers	272	2,281	11	134
Sewers	523	2,807	14	824
Shoemaking machine oper.	166	1,133	6	16
Solderers	111	802	4	63
Stationery firemen	186	2,172	11	44
	64	513	3	19
	55	863	4	18
Textiles operatives	447	3,839	19	26
	82	524	3	33
	286	1,983	10	111
Welders	1,640	16,348	82	395
Winding operatives	164	1,536	8	60
Machine operatives (n.e.c.)	2,538	23,383	117	1,232
Machine operatives (n.e.c.)	425	3,769	19	283
Misc. operatives	913	7,766	38	717
Not spec. operatives	311	2,283	11	97
Transport equipment operatives				
Busdrivers	146	1,811	9	118
*Urban transit workers	34	303	1	0
Deliverymen	520	5,342	27	333
Fork lift operatives	749	8,197	41	290
*Motormen	24	193	1	0
Parking attendents	86	1,050	5	53
Railroad brakemen	94	1,721	9	13
Railroad switchmen	49	434	2	0
Taxicab drivers	108	1,662	8	170
Truck drivers	3,841	46,198	230	1,035
Laborers, except farm				
Animal caretakers	58	362	2	27
Carpenters helpers	32	421	2	115
Construction laborers	868	8,740	44	1,266
Fishermen	2	14	0	103
Freight handlers	1,176	12,634	63	865

TABLE 4.3 (*continued*)

Occupation	Number Working Overtime for Premium Pay	Overtime Hours Worked for Premium Pay/Week	New Full-time Jobs Created	Experienced Unemployed
Garbage collectors	111	1,383	7	133
Gardeners	209	3,035	15	421
Longshoremen	48	951	5	11
Lumbermen	22	140	1	105
Stockhandlers	904	7,168	36	553
Vehicle washers	164	1,795	9	184
Warehouse men (n.e.c.)	442	4,082	20	196
Misc. Laborers	318	2,309	12	289
Not spec. laborers	407	6,546	33	387
Farmers and farm managers				
Farm managers	25	345	2	4
Farm laborers and farm foreman				
Farm foremen	21	413	2	18
Farm laborers	213	4,427	22	762
Service workers, except private household				
Chambermaids	39	442	2	398
Cleaners	241	2,717	14	794
Janitors	708	6,434	32	1,029
Bartenders	148	1,482	7	225
Busboys	33	196	1	265
Cooks	453	4,333	22	919
Dishwashers	22	26	0	402
Food counter attend.	73	859	4	530
Waiters	163	2,712	14	1,446
Food service workers (n.e.c.)	123	982	5	403
Health aides	76	1,110	6	153
Nursing aides	443	3,864	19	807
Practical nurses	217	1,980	10	228
Attendents	21	168	1	309
Attendents (n.e.c.)	18	146	1	117
Child care workers	48	907	5	351
Hairdressers	18	148	1	168
Housekeepers	81	509	3	94
Ushers	16	657	3	0
Firemen	107	2,327	12	23
Guards and watchmen	486	6,189	31	217
Police and detectives	560	6,069	30	81
Sheriffs and bailiffs	115	993	5	16
Private household workers				
Private housekeepers	22	87	0	99

Source: Authors' calculations from the May 1978 *CPS*.

Notes: 0 denotes fewer than 50.

    * Occupations for which the number of jobs created exceeds the number of unemployed.

TABLE 4.4
Experienced Unemployed and
Estimated Number of New Jobs Created by
Conversion of 20 Percent of Overtime,
by Major Craftsmen and Operative Occupational Group
and Geographic Division (× 100)

Occupation	New England	Middle Atlantic	East North Central	West North Central	South Atlantic	East South Central	West South Central	Mountain	Pacific
Carpenters									
Unemployed	14	158	141	15	129	12	19	49	133
Jobs created	8	3	4	4	9	2	4	5	5
Other construction craftsmen									
Unemployed	118	414	229	39	306	83	92	55	389
Jobs created	4	19	37	10	31	16	40	8	11
Foremen (n.e.c.)									
Unemployed	0	105	20	10	60	82	44	17	32
Jobs created	11	12	46	11	21	9	12	5	19
Machinists and job setters									
Unemployed	0	74	86	9	0	13	0	14	33
Jobs created	9	21	25	1	7	7	13	0	8
Metal craftsmen									
Unemployed	8	147	93	0	0	37	0	10	4
Jobs created	6	5	42	8	8	5	3	1	5
Mechanics, auto									
Unemployed	23	54	33	54	44	15	0	3	70
Jobs created	3	10	23	3	8	2	9	4	4

Occupation	New England	Middle Atlantic	East North Central	West North Central	South Atlantic	East South Central	West South Central	Mountain	Pacific
Mechanics, other than auto									
Unemployed	18	60	145	4	22	15	72	13	132
Jobs created	8	28	51	11	48	15	28	8	23
All other craftsmen									
Unemployed	53	237	104	46	37	18	24	33	309
Jobs created	8	14	30	14	26	10	21	15	30
Operatives, mine workers									
Unemployed	0	0	17	0	23	12	33	44	29
Jobs created	2	7	3	2	2	11	19	6	4
Operatives, motor vehicle equipment									
Unemployed	0	19	189	17	0	40	16	0	0
Jobs created	0	16	49	0	8	10	1	0	6
Operatives, other durable goods									
Unemployed	210	812	704	181	455	208	163	70	646
Jobs created	32	41	108	19	28	14	42	11	46
Operatives, nondurable goods									
Unemployed	154	732	460	98	614	373	250	95	587
Jobs created	16	16	49	15	55	18	23	11	8
All other operatives									
Unemployed	84	401	402	105	372	142	282	77	369
Jobs created	7	6	25	12	23	15	17	3	18

Source: Authors' calculations from the May 1978 *CPS*.
Note: 0 denotes fewer than 50.

TABLE 4.5
Experienced Unemployed and Estimated Number of New Jobs Created by Conversion of 20 Percent of Overtime, by Selected Detailed Craftsmen and Operative Occupations and Geographic Division (× 100)

Occupation	New England	Middle Atlantic	East North Central	West North Central	South Atlantic	East South Central	West South Central	Mountain	Pacific
Carpenters (4,337/0)									
Unemployed	1,424	15,769	12,426	1,526	12,888	1,215	1,862	4,851	13,282
Jobs Created	795	261	434	382	853	237	446	475	455
Cranemen et al. (2,700/1,770)									
Unemployed	0	2,034	1,635	0	0	0	0	403	1,916
Jobs Created	52	200	337	127	474	619	498	0	393
Electricians (6,655/2,388)									
Unemployed	0	5,934	1,614	230	5,053	0	0	0	5,310
Jobs Created	231	869	1,356	16	1,585	742	1,187	228	439
Excavating machine Operators (3,178/1,791)									
Unemployed	0	3,550	4,394	0	1,988	0	0	793	1,511
Jobs Created	18	254	440	332	276	519	922	335	81
Foremen (n.e.c.) (14,484/3,848)									
Unemployed	0	10,540	2,005	1,029	5,987	8,171	4,366	1,737	3,242
Jobs Created	1,057	1,159	4,660	1,155	2,087	835	1,157	453	1,872

TABLE 4.5 (continued)

Occupation	New England	Middle Atlantic	East North Central	West North Central	South Atlantic	East South Central	West South Central	Mountain	Pacific
Machinists (7,039/3,174)									
Unemployed	0	7,448	6,925	0	0	0	0	1,439	3,322
Jobs Created	845	1,800	1,461	133	623	513	1060	39	561
Mechanics, auto (6,465/1,112)									
Unemployed	2,332	5,360	3,259	4,456	4,446	0	0	326	4,908
Jobs Created	333	944	2,323	250	769	233	793	412	408
Mechanics, Heavy equipment (13,360/3,678)									
Unemployed	0	2,004	7,064	379	574	1,516	3,357	0	2,052
Jobs Created	499	1,340	3,940	548	3,054	1,201	891	528	1,357
Misc. mechanics (2,220/1,222)									
Unemployed	0	2,184	1,685	0	0	0	1,870	0	1,840
Jobs Created	176	196	366	8	696	285	314	57	122
Plumbers (3,298/934)									
Unemployed	5,900	10,449	1,209	1,133	6,408	0	0	465	10,259
Jobs Created	0	357	91	189	422	40	894	136	346
Telephone installers and repairmen (4,003/4,003)									
Unemployed	0	0	0	0	0	0	0	0	0
Jobs Created	0	357	561	117	478	234	533	902	733
Tool and die makers (3,746/1,180)									
Unemployed	0	4,590	2,811	0	0	0	0	0	0
Jobs Created	269	201	2,364	228	444	87	60	0	92

TABLE 4.5 (continued)

Occupation	New England	Middle Atlantic	East North Central	West North Central	South Atlantic	East South Central	West South Central	Mountain	Pacific
Assemblers (7,621/183)									
Unemployed	2,873	10,062	30,393	6,010	7,402	8,137	6,026	0	23,179
Jobs Created	631	543	3,427	384	789	141	209	183	1,156
Checkers (6,505/0)									
Unemployed	3,043	15,204	7,967	2,013	10,546	9,450	3,401	1,851	2,953
Jobs Created	631	543	2,136	473	801	718	594	48	561
Cutting operatives (2,099/214)									
Unemployed	869	6,225	5,595	219	2,829	0	0	1,446	3,495
Jobs Created	216	652	334	88	180	0	214	108	305
Mine operatives (n.e.c.) (4,290/838)									
Unemployed	0	0	1,736	0	2,293	1,155	3,251	3,414	111
Jobs Created	16	509	118	108	185	942	1,729	366	316
Grinding machine operators (2,071/1,105)									
Unemployed	0	0	7,223	4,290	0	0	0	0	1,785
Jobs Created	211	394	964	0	129	288	47	37	0
Punch press operators (2,208/566)									
Unemployed	2,468	1,516	1,515	0	0	0	0	253	4,004
Jobs Created	80	187	874	50	62	230	224	240	261
Welders (8,174/97)									
Unemployed	0	5,895	7,614	1,245	6,376	1,832	6,829	2,206	7,472
Jobs Created	97	1,060	2,676	922	641	583	1,145	314	738

TABLE 4.5 (continued)

Occupation	New England	Middle Atlantic	East North Central	West North Central	South Atlantic	East South Central	West South Central	Mountain	Pacific
Machine operatives (n.e.c.) (11,691/0)									
Unemployed	7,371	22,342	23,164	5,252	16,562	11,847	18,039	2,953	15,648
Jobs Created	1,030	1,164	3,876	333	978	1,244	1,696	541	827
Misc. operatives (3,883/0)									
Unemployed	948	20,125	9,702	3,133	14,194	3,032	2,450	2,810	15,245
Jobs Created	207	725	687	205	560	206	542	160	591

Source: Authors' calculations from the May 1978 *CPS*.
Notes: Occupations selected were those for which at least 2,000 jobs would be created nationwide.

Total number of jobs created for these occupations was 120,027.

Excess of new jobs over experienced unemployed in region/occupation cells where *Jobs created-Unemployed* is greater than zero is 28,103.

In parentheses are shown the sum of new jobs created/ the sum, over those regions where *Jobs Created-Unemployed* is greater than zero, of the excess of jobs created over the unemployed.

5 · COMPLIANCE WITH THE OVERTIME PAY PROVISIONS OF THE FLSA

Although analyses of the effects of labor market legislation typically assume that the legislation is fully complied with, noncompliance is always a potential problem.[1] The simulated gains in employment that would result from an increase in the overtime premium presented in Chapter 2 assumed full compliance with the legislation. This is not a realistic assumption, and less than perfect compliance will reduce the potential employment gain associated with an increase in the overtime premium. Furthermore, since an increase in the overtime premium would increase the amount employers save by not complying with the legislation, such an increase might lead to a further reduced compliance rate. This would further moderate the actual decline in overtime hours and increase in employment that resulted from an increase in the overtime premium (although noncompliance or increased noncompliance would also reduce the disemployment effects of a higher premium discussed in Chapter 3).

A number of data sources provide some information on compliance with overtime legislation. A U.S. Department of Labor compliance survey conducted in 1965 indicated that 30 percent of the establishments in which overtime was worked were in violation of the overtime provisions of the FLSA and 5.9 percent of the employ-

---

1. A recent study that explicitly considers the question of compliance is Ashenfelter and Smith 1979.

ees working overtime were not paid in accordance with the overtime provisions (see table 5.1). More recently, Department of Labor investigations of complaints of violations under the FLSA in fiscal year 1977 found a greater dollar volume of violations of the overtime pay provisions than of the minimum wage provisions (U.S., Department of Labor 1978). Finally, data from the annual May supplements to the *Current Population Survey* (*CPS*) indicate that during the period from 1973 to 1978, less than 43 percent of full-time wage and salary workers who worked forty-one or more hours a week at one job reported receiving premium pay (Stamas 1979, p. 41). While many of these individuals may work in noncovered employment, these *CPS* data do suggest that noncompliance with the overtime premium provisions may be a sizable problem. Of course, as table 1.1 indicates, only 58 percent of all wage and salary workers are covered by the overtime provisions of the FLSA. Since one may reasonably conjecture that noncovered workers are more likely to work overtime, as these noncovered workers' marginal costs of overtime hours are lower than those of otherwise identical covered workers, the *CPS* data cited should be considered only suggestive.

Knowledge of the correlates of noncompliance may well be as important to policy makers as knowledge of the rate of noncompliance. If noncompliance is found to be widespread, policy makers may decide to push for an increase in the resources devoted to compliance investigations and also for an increase in the penalties for noncompliance. Knowledge of the correlates can serve as a guide to the allocation of the limited resources the government has to assure compliance. Moreover, information on the relationship among compliance and various explanatory variables may shed some light on the question of whether increasing the overtime premium will lead to an increase in the noncompliance rate.

New Estimates of Noncompliance

The May 1978 *CPS* contained data on 11,738 individuals who reported that they worked forty-one or more hours during the survey week for a single employer. It would be incorrect, however, to focus on this entire sample when discussing compliance with the overtime pay provisions since there are numerous individuals who are not subject to the provisions (see Appendix C). These include, but are not restricted to, supervisory employees, outside salespersons, employees in seasonal industries (including agriculture), state and local government employees, employees in small retail trade and service sector establishments, and some household workers.

Fortunately, it is possible to assign each individual who worked overtime to one of three groups: those who are definitely subject to the overtime pay provisions, those who are subject to the provisions with a known probability, and those who are not subject to the provisions or for whom coverage probabilities can not be determined. The assignment is based upon an algorithm that makes use of knowledge of the various exemptions to the overtime provisions of the FLSA and of the detailed three-digit census industry and occupation categories in which each individual is employed. In the case of individuals employed in retail trade and selected service industries in which coverage under the overtime provisions was based upon whether the establishment's sales exceeded $250,000 per year in 1978, each individual was assigned a probability of coverage equal to the fraction of employees in the three-digit industry who worked in establishments with sales of greater than $250,000 in 1977.[2] The latter information came from published volumes of the *1977 Census of Retail Trade, 1977 Census of Selected Service Industries,* and unpublished tabulations specially prepared for this research by the Bureau of the Census.

Details of the algorithm used to assign individuals to the three groups are contained in Appendix C. As table 5.2 indicates, the procedure resulted in the classification of 4,331 individuals as being definitely subject to the overtime pay provisions and 944 individuals as being subject to the provisions with known probability. It is these two groups, which represent 45.0 percent of the individuals who reported working overtime, that are the focus of the remainder of this chapter; and often, the subsequent analyses restrict the sample further to those individuals who reported they were paid on an

---

2. The establishment sales size test rose to $275,000 on July 1, 1978, and has increased still further since then; however, since the *CPS* data is for May 1978, the $250,000 figure is the correct one to use.

hourly basis. This reduces the samples to 3,231 and 535 individuals respectively, some 32 percent of the original sample.

Individuals in the *CPS* sample reported whether they received any premium pay for overtime hours in excess of forty per week, not what their overtime pay premium was. While it is possible to construct an estimate of the overtime pay premium for a subset of individuals in the sample, as follows, this estimate is subject to considerable error. Because of this, noncompliance is defined in three different ways in this section.

First, noncompliance is defined as failure to receive *any* premium pay for hours of work beyond forty hours per week. Since receipt of a premium of less than time and a half represents noncompliance also, such a definition clearly understates the extent of noncompliance. Second, for the subset of people who reported their usual weekly earnings U, usual weekly hours H, and usual hourly earnings W, the overtime premium P is estimated by

$$P = (U - 40W)/(H - 40)W, \tag{5.1}$$

and noncompliance can then be defined as failure to receive an estimated premium of at least time and a half ($P < 1.5$); the computation in 5.1 assumes that reported usual weekly earnings *include* overtime pay, that reported usual hourly earnings *exclude* overtime pay, and that the overtime premium goes into effect after forty hours. Finally, to see how sensitive the results are to a slightly lower bound and to allow for the possibility of rounding errors in the calculations, failure to receive an estimated premium of at least 1.4 is considered as an alternative measure of noncompliance.[3]

Table 5.3 focuses on the individuals who are definitely subject to the overtime pay provisions of the FLSA and, weighting each observation by its sample weight, computes the various estimates of noncompliance; these are found in the first column. When noncom-

---

3. These definitions of compliance ignore the fact that the existence of the overtime pay premium may have caused some employers, who otherwise would have worked their workforces overtime, to avoid the use of overtime. Such employers would be complying with the legislation, but individuals employed in these firms would not be included in the sample. Although the next section returns to this point when it attempts to estimate whether government resources devoted to increasing compliance reduce the probability that an individual will work overtime, it should be understood that noncompliance is defined in this section to be conditional on individuals working overtime.

pliance is defined as failure to receive any premium pay for overtime, 23.3 percent of the individuals in the sample fell in this category. The estimate of the noncompliance rate of 23.3 percent is
considerably higher than the estimate of 5.9 percent obtained in the
1965 BLS compliance survey.

It is possible, however, that the three-digit census occupational codes that were used in the algorithm to determine coverage
under the overtime pay provisions may not be sufficiently narrow to
always enable correct classification of these workers as being subject
to the legislation. Section 13(a)(1) of the FLSA exempts from coverage "any employee employed in a bona fide executive (or) administrative . . . capacity." Some three-digit occupational categories included in the sample may be sufficiently wide that they include a
number of supervisory employees who are exempt from the legislation. For example, the three-digit occupation "telephone operator"
includes not only operators but also supervisors of operators, and
the latter *may* be considered administrative personnel for the purposes of the FLSA. The inclusion of such individuals in the sample
would give this estimate of noncompliance an upward bias.

Although there is no way to fully control for this possibility
because the three-digit occupational category is the smallest division
reported, a partial solution is to restrict the sample to workers paid
on an hourly basis since it is unlikely that these employees would be
exempt from the overtime provisions. Item 2 of table 5.3 shows that,
when the conservative definition of noncompliance is applied to this
hourly wage sample, the estimate of noncompliance falls to 9.6 percent. And, as item 3 shows, when the conservative definition of
noncompliance is applied to the more restricted sample of hourly
wage workers for whom an overtime premium can be computed, the
estimate of noncompliance is also 9.6 percent. Although these estimates of noncompliance are less than the previous estimate of 23.3
percent, they are still higher than the 1965 *BLS* estimate of 5.9
percent.

Table 5.3 also shows that when equation 5.1 is used to calculate the actual premium received for the restricted sample of hourly
wage workers for whom an overtime premium can be computed, the
estimate of noncompliance is dramatically higher than any of the
previous estimates. In item 4, where noncompliance is defined as

failure to receive a premium of at least 1.5 of usual hourly earnings, the estimate of noncompliance is 73.3 percent. Finally, item 5 shows that even when noncompliance is defined as failure to receive a premium of at least 1.4 of usual hourly earnings, the estimate of noncompliance only falls to 64.8 percent.

These data suggest that noncompliance with the overtime pay premium provisions may be fairly widespread. Indeed, it is worth emphasizing that this initial sample excludes industries in which there are size-class exemptions and occupations in which coverage is incomplete. One might speculate that noncompliance would be higher in these industries and occupations, since employees' knowledge of their rights to receive overtime premiums of time and a half and employers' knowledge of that obligation to pay such premiums may both be lower in such situations. A test of this speculation follows.

The 9.6 percent estimate of noncompliance obtained when noncompliance was defined to be failure to receive any premium pay for overtime hours greater than forty is a conservative lower bound estimate. The estimates obtained using the estimated overtime premiums, however, seem excessively high. It is doubtful that 65 to 73 percent of all employees who should be receiving time and a half for overtime are not. Of course, the assumptions that underlie the calculation in 5.1 must be kept in mind. If usual weekly earnings U fail to include all overtime earnings or if usual hourly earnings W include some or all overtime earnings, then the premium will be understated by equation 5.1. In contrast, if not all overtime hours are included in usual weekly hours H or the overtime premium goes into effect before forty hours a week (due perhaps to a collective bargaining agreement), then the premium will be overstated by equation 5.1. The *CPS* questionnaire gives no guidance as to which, if any, of these situations occur. Given the magnitude of the estimates of noncompliance obtained, however, it is likely that the first set of biases dominate.

Some support for this view comes from a parallel analysis of data from the 1977 Michigan *Quality of Employment Survey (QES)*.[4]

---

4. Additional support is provided by Carstenen and Woltman 1979, who contrasted survey results from the January 1977 *CPS* and a survey of *CPS* respondents' employers. They found that, as compared with the employer responses, indi-

The *QES* is a sample of more than fifteen hundred employed adults, and the premium received for overtime work was explicitly reported for those individuals who worked overtime. Unfortunately, most adults in the survey failed to work overtime, and after applying the algorithm to isolate those individuals who were subject to the legislation with certainty (including the restriction that they were paid on an hourly basis), the sample was reduced to only sixty-nine individuals. Of these individuals, however, almost 16 percent failed to receive a premium of time and a half; this number falls to 14.5 percent if noncompliance is defined to be receipt of a premium of less than 1.4 straight-time wages (table 5.3, third column).

Because of the small sample size involved in this calculation, one cannot place too much faith in the specific value of the estimate. Nevertheless, it does suggest that the actual noncompliance rate in the complete coverage sector is probably closer to the lower bound estimate of 9.6 percent than it is to 65.0 or 70.0 percent. It should be reemphasized that the former figure refers to the fraction of those individuals working overtime who failed to receive any premium; it does not include those individuals who received overtime pay premiums of less than time and a half. To the extent that some individuals received premiums lower than that specified by the FLSA, the actual noncompliance rate will be above 9.6 percent.[5]

Turning next to those individuals employed in retail trade and selected service industries in which coverage is based on the employer's sales, it was not possible to directly estimate compliance because the *CPS* does not report the sales of the establishment in which each individual works. As was previously described, however,

---

viduals tended to overstate hours worked and understate hourly wages and usual weekly earnings. Since the percentage understatement in weekly earnings tended to be greater than that for hourly wages and both exceeded the percentage overstatement of usual hours, this would suggest that computations of the overtime premium using equation 5.1 would be biased downwards and cause an overstatement of the extent of noncompliance—assuming, of course that the employers' responses were correct.

5. One additional set of results warrant brief mention. Analyses discussed in the next section suggest that the noncompliance rate was higher in the federal sector than in the private sector. Some may find it inconceivable that federal government agencies would fail to comply uniformly with federal legislation. While we do not necessarily agree with this view, it is instructive to note that when the analyses exclude federal workers (table 5.3, second column), the results change only marginally.

it was possible to compute for each individual the probability that his or her employer's sales were above $250,000. This probability of coverage, together with the information on whether or not the individual received any overtime premium, or whether or not the individual received a premium of at least time and a half, allowed a more indirect method to be used to compute the noncompliance rate for this sample.

To illustrate this method, let C_i denote the probability of coverage for industry i. This is equal to the proportion of individuals in each of the retail trade and service industries who are employed in establishments with annual sales of at least $250,000. Let P_{ic} equal the probability that a worker subject to the overtime provisions in industry i who works overtime does *not* receive a premium in compliance with the legislation and P_{in} the comparable probability for workers not subject to the legislation. P_{ic} is in fact the noncompliance rate, the variable being estimated. The probability that an individual working overtime in industry i is not getting paid a premium in compliance with the legislation, P_{ia}, is given by

$$P_{ia} = P_{ic}C_i + P_{in}(1 - C_i) = P_{in} + (P_{ic} - P_{in})C_i. \tag{5.2}$$

This is nothing more than a weighted average of the noncompliance rates for the workers who are subject to and not subject to the legislation, with the weights being the proportion of workers subject to and not subject to the legislation.[6] Of course, for workers *not* subject to the legislation, the term noncompliance does not denote

---

6. Data limitations force the assumption in this calculation that the proportion of employees working overtime in an industry that is subject to the overtime pay provisions of the FLSA equals the reported proportion of employees in that industry who are subject to the provisions (C_i). This assumption may be inappropriate because the usage of overtime hours may vary systematically with establishment size (and hence coverage), although it appears impossible to specify the direction of this relationship. On the one hand, the usage of overtime may be higher in small establishments that are not subject to the legislation, because their marginal costs of overtime hours are lower. On the other hand, the size-class exemptions to the FLSA were instituted because small establishments were able to argue successfully that they did not regularly schedule overtime hours and that their usage of overtime occurred only in emergencies; if this argument is true, the proportionate usage of overtime would increase with establishment size. The implication of all this is that the proportion of employees in an industry working overtime that are subject to the overtime provisions may be measured here with some error; however, it is impossible to determine if this proportion is systematically overstated or understated.

any violation of law; it simply reflects failure to receive the premium called for by the law in the covered sector.

Now suppose initially that P_{ic} and P_{in} were constant across individuals and industries. That is, the probabilities that workers working overtime, either subject to or not subject to the overtime pay provisions of the FLSA, fail to receive a premium in accordance with the legislation do not vary with the characteristics of the individual or the industry. In this case, equation 5.2 can be written

$$P_{ia} = P_n + (P_c - P_n)C_i \tag{5.3}$$

where P_c and P_n are the constant noncompliance rates of workers subject to, and not subject to, the legislation respectively.

In this situation, it should be clear that if, for the sample of individuals working overtime, the simple linear probability function model is estimated by

$$d_{ij} = a_0 + a_1C_i + \epsilon \tag{5.4}$$

where d_{ij} takes on the value of 1 if individual j in industry i is not paid a premium in accordance with the legislation and the value of 0 if he or she is paid a premium, that the noncompliance rate for workers subject to the legislation can be estimated by

$$P_c = \hat{a}_0 + \hat{a}_1 \tag{5.5}$$

where $\hat{a}_0$ and $\hat{a}_1$ are the estimated values of a_0 and a_1.[7]

Of course, it is not likely that P_{ic} and P_{in} are constant across individuals or industries. The simplest modification is to assume that the probability of noncompliance in the covered sector varies with the proportion of individuals in the industry who are subject to the legislation. In particular, it might be argued that as this proportion increases the noncompliance rate will fall for those subject to the legislation, since both employees and employers will be more likely to be aware of their being subject to the legislation. In this case

$$P_{ic} = P_{c0} + P_{c1}C_i \qquad P_{c1} > 0 \tag{5.6a}$$

$$P_{in} = P_n \tag{5.6b}$$

---

7. While there are well-known statistical problems associated with the linear probability model, it is used here both for expository purposes and because the more appropriate probit or logit models would not permit the linear aggregation across workers subject to and not subject to the legislation that is necessary.

and substituting equations 5.6 into equation 5.2 yields

$$P_{ia} = P_n + (P_{c0} - P_n)C_i + P_{c1}C_i^2. \tag{5.7}$$

Consequently, if a linear probability function model of the following form is estimated

$$d_{ij} = b_0 + b_1C_i + b_2C_i^2, \tag{5.8}$$

the noncompliance rate in industry i can be obtained from

$$P_{ic} = \hat{b}_0 + \hat{b}_1 + \hat{b}_2C_i \tag{5.9}$$

where $\hat{b}_0$, $\hat{b}_1$, and $\hat{b}_2$ are the estimated values of the parameters in equation 5.8.[8]

It is a straightforward progression to generalize this methodology still further to allow for characteristics of the individual and other characteristics of the establishment in which the individual works to influence the probability of noncompliance. A vector of variables including the individual's age, sex, marital status, race, ethnic background, education, and union status are available in the *CPS* data, and the next section discusses why each of these variables might be expected to influence the probability of noncompliance. For now, suppose that these variables can be denoted by a vector **X** and that the probabilities of an individual j, who is employed in industry i, not receiving a premium in compliance with the overtime provisions are given, in the two sectors, by

$$P_{ijc} = P_{c0} + \mathbf{P}'_{c1}\mathbf{X_j} \tag{5.10a}$$

and

$$P_{ijn} = P_{n0} + \mathbf{P}'_{n1}\mathbf{X_j} \tag{5.10b}$$

respectively.

Substitution of equations 5.10 into equation 5.2 then yields the probability that an individual with characteristics $\mathbf{X_j}$ in industry i

---

8. It might be desirable to allow P_n to also vary with the proportion of employees subject to the legislation. For example, one might hypothesize that if labor markets are competitive, an increase in the proportion of workers subject to the legislation would increase the probability that employers not subject to the legislation would have to pay overtime premiums to attract workers. Unfortunately, if one allows P_n to vary with C, the resulting estimating equation would be underidentified. More precisely, one would arrive at equation 5.8 as the estimating equation, but one would not be able to recover estimates of P_{c0} and P_{c1} from that equation.

who is working overtime receives a premium in compliance with the legislation (P_{ija}) is given by

$$P_{ija} = P_{n0} + \mathbf{P}'_{n1}\mathbf{X}_j + (P_{c0} - P_{n0})C_i + (\mathbf{P}_{c1} - \mathbf{P}_{n1})' \, \mathbf{X}_j C_i \quad (5.11)$$

Hence, if one estimates the linear probability function model

$$d_{ij} = e_0 + e_1\mathbf{X}_j + e_2 C_i + e_3'\mathbf{X}_j C_i 0 + \epsilon \quad (5.12)$$

the *average* compliance rate for workers subject to the overtime pay provisions of the FLSA in these industries can be obtained from

$$P = (\hat{e}_0 + \hat{e}_2) + (\hat{\mathbf{e}}_1 + \hat{\mathbf{e}}_3)'\bar{\mathbf{X}} \quad (5.13)$$

where $\bar{\mathbf{X}}$ is the mean value of $\mathbf{X}$ for individuals in the sample who are subject to the legislation.[9] Generalizing this approach to allow P_{ijc} to vary with C_i is also straightforward.

Table 5.4 presents estimates of the proportion of employees subject to the overtime provisions of the FLSA (C_i) in May 1978 for thirty-six three-digit retail trade and service industries.[10] The proportion varied considerably across industries, ranging from 1.00 for department stores to only 0.04 for barber shops. There were 535 individuals in the May 1978 *CPS* sample who worked at least forty-one hours during the survey week and reported that they were paid by the hour, were not exempt from the overtime provisions for other reasons (such as being outside salespersons) and were employed in one of these industries. These individuals form the partial coverage sample.

Estimates of equations 5.4, 5.8, 5.12, and the generalization that allows the probability of noncompliance to vary both with the individual's characteristics $\mathbf{X}_j$ and the industry coverage rate C_i are found in appendix tables D.3 and D.4. The results in the former table do not allow the probability of noncompliance to vary with the coverage rate, while the results in the latter table do.

The implied estimates of noncompliance with the overtime pay provisions obtained from these results, using equations 5.5, 5.9, and 5.13, are found in table 5.5. In each case, noncompliance is

---

9. Actually one knows only the mean value of $\mathbf{X}$ for all individuals in the sample, and these are used instead in the calculations that follow.

10. These numbers should more precisely be interpreted as the proportion of employees who are not exempt for other reasons (e.g., who are not supervisory or outside salespersons) and who are subject to the overtime provisions.

defined as failure to receive *any* overtime pay premium; the estimates are therefore likely to understate the true noncompliance rate.

Quite strikingly, these estimates strongly suggest that noncompliance *is* higher for workers subject to the overtime provisions in the partially covered sample than it is in the complete coverage sample, as was earlier hypothesized. For example, using the simplest model that assumes that the probability of noncompliance does not vary with individual or industry characteristics, one obtains an estimate that, in the partially covered sample, 20.2 percent of individuals working overtime and subject to the overtime pay provisions failed to receive any premium pay for overtime (table 5.5, model 1). When the model is generalized to allow noncompliance to vary with characteristics of the individual, the noncompliance rate, evaluated at the mean values of the characteristics, rises to 24.5 percent (table 5.5, model 2). These estimates are substantially higher than the 9.6 percent estimate of noncompliance observed in the complete coverage *CPS* sample.

It is also possible to compute estimates of the proportion of individuals in the sample who are not subject to the overtime pay provisions and who did not receive any overtime pay premium for overtime hours. These estimated noncompliance rates have no normative significance, as these workers are not legally required to receive a premium. Nonetheless, it is interesting to note that they are considerably larger than the noncompliance rates for workers in these industries subject to the legislation. Indeed, the estimates of "noncompliance" for workers in this sample not subject to the FLSA is 64.2 percent when the probability of receiving a premium is assumed not to vary with individuals' characteristics and 48.5 percent when it is assumed to vary (table 5.5).

It is tempting to conclude from these estimates that a reasonable estimate of the effect of the FLSA on the probability that workers in these industries who *are* subject to the overtime provisions are paid a premium is the difference between the proportions receiving premium pay in both sectors. The estimates would imply then that the FLSA has increased the probability that a worker receives premium pay for overtime by between 24.0 (48.5−24.5) and 44.0 (64.2−20.2) percentage points.

Such a conclusion would be incorrect for at least two reasons. First, the presence of a covered sector may well affect the probability that establishments in the noncovered sector pay premium pay; the problem here is analogous to that of estimating of union members' wages relative to the wages of comparable nonunion workers, which tells very little about the effect of unions on their members' absolute wage levels. Second, there is no reason to presume that the probability that noncovered (small) establishments pay a premium is an accurate estimate of the probability that covered (larger) establishments would pay an overtime premium, in the absence of the legislation. The present estimates simply can not be used to infer anything about the quantitative effect of the FLSA on the proportion of workers receiving premium pay for overtime in this sector.

Finally, the estimates in table D.4 can be used to compute estimates of the noncompliance rate, at the mean value of C in the sample, under the assumption that noncompliance in the covered sector varies with the industry coverage ratio. These estimates are found in the last two rows of table 5.5, and they suggest considerably higher noncompliance rates for workers subject to the legislation than do the first two rows. These latter results should not be taken too seriously, however, for as indicated in table 5.5, the estimates also imply *negative* noncompliance rates among workers not subject to the FLSA overtime provisions—that is, they imply that more than 100 percent of the people working overtime received premium pay, a logical impossibility. To recover estimates of noncompliance in this model, it was necessary to assume that the proportion of employees in an industry covered by the FLSA did not affect the probability that premium pay was received for overtime in the noncovered sector. If increases in coverage do increase the probability that premium pay is received in the noncovered sector, the estimates of P_c in models 3 and 4 will be biased up and those of P_n biased down. Noncompliance may well vary with coverage rates, but unfortunately it is not possible to identify the relationship.

Determinants of Noncompliance

What are the factors that influence the probability that an individual who is working overtime and subject to the overtime pay provisions of the FLSA is not being paid, in compliance with the legislation, a premium of at least time and a half? An economic model of noncompliance would start from the proposition that an employer's decision not to comply with the legislation is based on the benefits and the costs that he or she believes are associated with noncompliance.[11] The benefits from noncompliance are the savings that accrue to the employer from failing to pay workers in compliance with the legislation. The costs of noncompliance include the costs to the employer of any increased employee turnover that may result from failure to pay legally required premium payments. These costs are likely to be higher for skilled workers than they are for unskilled workers and higher for workers the employer expects or wants to have long job tenure than they are for workers with short expected job tenure.

The costs of noncompliance also include any costs that would result if an employer is caught violating the overtime pay provisions; these costs are determined both by the probability of being caught if a violation occurs and the expected penalty once a violation is identified. The resources available to the Employment Standards Administration (ESA) to enforce the provisions of the FLSA are minimal and only rarely does the agency initiate investigations on its own (see Ashenfelter and Smith 1979 for background data). More typically, investigations result from alleged violations being reported by employees who believe that they have not been paid in accordance with the provisions of the act. This suggests that the costs of noncompliance that an employer perceives will increase as his or her perception that an employee will report a violation increases. It also increases with the employer's expectation that such a report will be investigated.

Finally, the costs an employer perceives are associated with noncompliance depend upon the expected penalty once a violation is judged to occur. Since the penalty for first-time violators who do not falsify their records involves only back payment of the premium pay that is owed to workers (without interest) and the typical settlement involves repayment of substantially less than 100 percent of the funds owed, the incentives for firms to comply with the legisla-

---

11. The work in this section draws heavily on that of Ashenfelter and Smith 1979.

tion are not very high. For example, in fiscal year 1977, Department of Labor investigations discovered $88 million of overtime pay premium violations, but only $33 million of this total was repaid to workers (U.S., Department of Labor 1978, p. 21).

It should not be surprising then to have obtained lower bound estimates of noncompliance of roughly 10 percent in the completely covered sector and 20 percent in the partially covered sector. Indeed, the fact that the noncompliance rate is not substantially higher suggests that while calculations of the benefits and costs from noncompliance influence employers' decisions, they are not the sole determinant. Other factors, such as the desire to obey government legislation, clearly are important.

It is possible to formalize these ideas by asserting that an employer's decision not to comply with the overtime provisions of the FLSA is at least partially determined by the net benefits (benefits B − costs C) that the employer perceives he or she will receive from noncompliance. Other things being equal, as these net benefits increase, the probability of the employer's noncompliance P_c will increase:

$$P_c = F(B - C) \qquad F' > 0 \tag{5.14}$$

Hence, anything that increases the net benefits from noncompliance should increase the probability of noncompliance.

The present data on noncompliance are for individuals, and it is logical to ask what variables influence the probability that a worker subject to the overtime provisions of the FLSA and working overtime does not receive premium pay in compliance with the legislation. Table 5.6 lists a set of variables, for which data are available for the individuals in the CPS and QES samples or which can be constructed from other sources, that might be expected to influence the net benefits an employer would receive from noncompliance.

The noncompliance rate is expected to first decline and then to increase with employee age. Teenagers have high expected turnover rates, which makes it unlikely that employers will heavily invest in their training and thus that any increase in their turnover rates due to noncompliance would be costly to the firm. As new entrants, teenagers are also less likely to be aware of the overtime provisions of the FLSA, and this, along with their high turnover rates, makes it unlikely that they would report any violation to the ESA. As such, the noncompliance rate will likely be high for teenagers.

As individuals age and develop long-standing attachment to firms, they accumulate both considerable firm-specific knowledge and knowledge of the FLSA's provisions. Noncompliance with the overtime provisions for these individuals will be costly for the firm; it would be costly to replace them if they quit, and the probability that a FLSA violation will be reported by them is high. After some period, however, workers become locked in; their earnings with their current employer exceed their earnings potential elsewhere due to the firm-specific knowledge they have accumulated. This reduces the probability that they will quit in response to noncompliance, which reduces the costs of noncompliance that employers face. These arguments suggest that the noncompliance rate should first decline and then increase with age.

Turning next to the role of an employee's sex, there are two conflicting forces at work. On the one hand, females have historically had higher turnover rates and shorter expected tenure than males, and thus they received less firm-specific training. This implies that any noncompliance-induced quits by them would be less costly to firms than quits by males; as a result noncompliance rates for females might be expected to be higher than those for males. On the other hand, in a period of increasing litigation, employers may be concerned that failure to pay females the legally required premiums would lead to the possibility of sex discrimination suits; this should reduce the noncompliance rate for females. The net effect of these two forces is indeterminate.

Discrimination against nonwhites or Hispanics may manifest itself in higher noncompliance probabilities for individuals from these groups. The fact that some Hispanics are not fluent in English and thus may not be fully aware of the legislation reinforces this effect, as does the possibility that some may be undocumented workers who would be unlikely to complain to authorities about violations of the FLSA. (It is, however, highly unlikely that any undocumented workers would be represented in the *CPS* sample.) Of course, fear of litigation, or government compliance activities on behalf of nonwhites, might reduce the noncompliance rates for that group.

Highly skilled individuals are likely both to be costly for firms to replace if they quit and also to be fully aware of their legal rights. As such, higher educational levels should be associated with lower noncompliance rates, other things being equal. Individuals earning high wages, other things equal, are also likely to have the same characteristics. Here, however, the firm also has an incentive not to comply, since as an individual's wage rate increases, the benefits or premium savings from noncompliance also increase. On balance, one might expect that the former effect dominates and that noncompliance will decline as wage rates increase. Put another way, in structured internal labor markets in which high-wage employees have implicit or explicit long-term contracts, noncompliance, if known, might lead to a reduced supply of new applicants. This would bid up the straight-time wage the firm would have to offer, offsetting any benefits from noncompliance.

Noncompliance is also expected to be lower in unionized environments than in nonunion environments. One important role of unions is to monitor employees' working conditions to assure that both collectively bargained and legally required conditions of employment are satisfied. Not only do unions call violations of legal requirements to the attention of employers, but they are less reluctant than individual employees—since they fear retribution less—to call these violations to the attention of enforcement agencies.

The *CPS* and *QES* data contain information on the industry in which each individual is employed. Other things equal, one should expect that noncompliance rates will be lower in highly concentrated industries. Firms in concentrated industries, which face relatively inelastic product demand curves, can increase their product prices when faced with paying an overtime premium, without fear of losing all their sales. This reduces the benefits of noncompliance. In contrast, a firm in a highly competitive industry has little control over product price and, faced with the legal requirement to pay an overtime premium, may achieve greater benefits from noncompliance.

Finally, noncompliance can be expected to be lower in areas in which greater resources are devoted by the government to assuring compliance with the Fair Labor Standards Act, since the probability of violations being caught should be higher in such areas.[12] The ESA provided data on the total number of FLSA compliance actions undertaken and the total FLSA compliance budget for each of the ninety local ESA area offices in 1978. These data enabled the aggregation up to state totals and the merging into each *CPS* individual's record of data on these two measures of compliance, each deflated by the number of private and federal nonsupervisory workers in the state in order to approximate resources expanded per worker subject to the legislation.[13]

Appendix tables D.1 and D.2 present estimates of probit models for the sample of workers who are definitely subject to the overtime pay provisions of the FLSA for the 1978 May *CPS* and 1977 *QES* data respectively. Noncompliance is defined in the former data set to be failure to receive any premium for overtime hours worked in excess of forty per week, while in the latter it is defined to be failure to receive a premium of at least time and a half. One should remember that the sample size in the latter case is extremely small (69 individuals), and thus it is unlikely that statistically signifi-

---

12. All the previously mentioned hypothesized effects, save for that of race, assume that government resources devoted to compliance activity are randomly distributed. But if the government were trying to maximize the effectiveness of its compliance activities, it would assign them in such a way as to maximize the expected number of violations it would uncover (see Ashenfelter and Smith 1979 for an elaboration of this point). So for example, it would investigate primarily low-wage nonunion firms in competitive industries, where violations are likely to occur, rather than high-wage union firms in concentrated industries, in which violations are less likely to occur.

Clearly, such a rational assignment of government resources would reduce the chances of observing noncompliance being correlated with the other determinants that were postulated to be important; Ashenfelter and Smith did find some evidence that compliance resources were being assigned nonrandomly. Hence, the empirical estimates obtained should be understood to represent the product of the interactions between employer decisions and government assignment of enforcement resources. Of course, given the low level of government enforcement activity, it would be surprising to see it substantially alter the pattern (as opposed to the level) of noncompliance.

13. The state level was the finest geographic breakdown that could be identified in the *CPS* data. Since some local offices served more than one state, it was often necessary to aggregate data across several states. As a result, the number of individual states, or state aggregates, for which these totals could be computed is actually thirty-two. Also, it is impossible to separate the resources devoted to minimum wage and overtime pay violation activities from each other.

cant relationships will be observed in those data. Nevertheless, since empirical regularities are less subject to challenge when they are replicated in different data bases, both sets of estimates are presented.

The dependent variable in the probit model in each case is a dichotomous variable that takes on the value of 1 if the individual failed to receive a premium in compliance with the legislation and 0 otherwise. The explanatory variables in the case of the *CPS* data were those described above, as well as several others. In both data sets, a set of dichotomous variables are included to capture the effect of the major (one-digit) industry group in which the individual is employed. Only a subset of the other explanatory variables were available in the *QES*. In particular, since state of residence was not reported in this survey, resources devoted to compliance activities in the state could not be included in the analyses.

The signs of the estimated coefficients from these models are summarized in the first and second columns of table 5.6; an asterisk next to a sign indicates that the underlying coefficient or coefficients proved to be statistically significantly different from zero at conventional levels of significance. Quite strikingly, a number of the hypotheses are borne out. Furthermore, none of the coefficients that are statistically significant are opposite in sign to that expected.

For example, both data bases indicate quite clearly that noncompliance rates are significantly lower in firms in which unions are present than they are in nonunion firms. Similarly, the probability of noncompliance is significantly lower in heavily concentrated industries, such as manufacturing and public utilities, than it is in less concentrated industries such as mining, construction, wholesale trade, and finance, insurance, and real estate. Finally, the probability of noncompliance is significantly negatively related to an individual's earnings level in the *CPS* data.

Other results are supportive of the model, although less clear cut. An increase in the level of government resources devoted to compliance activities in a state does appear to reduce the probability of noncompliance; however, this variable is statistically insignificant. The probability of noncompliance is significantly higher for nonwhites than whites in the *QES* data, suggesting that discrimination is present and that this effect dominates any effect of government enforcement activity. Noncompliance is also seen to increase with employee age. Additional results suggest this relationship occurs primarily for older workers; other things equal, the probability of noncompliance appears to be some 4 to 6 percent higher for workers older than age fifty-five than for all other workers. As hypothesized earlier, to the extent that mobility of older workers is limited, older workers may be less likely to initiate complaints about nonreceipt of premium pay. Contrary to expectations, however, alternative specifications provided no evidence that noncompliance rates were also higher for teenagers.[14]

Taken together, these results provide strong support for the view that at least some employers do make conscious decisions about whether to comply with the overtime provisions of the FLSA, decisions that involve a balancing of the benefits and the costs of such an action.[15] Further support for this view can be found from the analyses of the sector in which workers' coverage under the overtime pay provisions of the FLSA can be determined with only a known probability. The relevant model in this case is given by equations 5.10, 5.11, and 5.12 where X_j is the vector of explanatory variables associated with the worker (these are found in appendix table D.1). Estimates of the linear probability model 5.12 are found in appendix

14. In all these investigations, compliance is defined as conditional on the individual's working overtime. The existence of the overtime premium and efforts to enforce compliance with the premium, however, may reduce the probability that individuals actually work overtime. If this occurs, the estimates in appendix tables D.1 and D.2 may be subject to sample selection bias; they may confound the effect of an explanatory variable on the probability of noncompliance with its effect on the probability of working overtime (see Heckman 1979).

Using data on individuals in the *CPS* who both did and did not work overtime, attempts were made to correct for this problem by estimating a model in which the probability of working overtime and the probability of not receiving a premium were simultaneously determined. Unfortunately, such an approach yielded very few significant coefficients, probably because it is a difficult model to accurately specify. In any case, no evidence was found that increasing the resources devoted to compliance activity will decrease the probability that individuals work overtime.

15. This might suggest to some that an increase in the overtime premium would lead to an increased noncompliance rate. But an increase in the overtime premium also increases employees' economic incentives to report noncompliance, and the increased threat of such actions on their parts may induce employers to reduce the noncompliance rate. Since the penalties for noncompliance are virtually zero for first offenders, it seems highly unlikely that this latter effect would overwhelm the former. There is no firm evidence on this point, however.

table D.3, and the implied marginal effects of each of the explanatory variables on the compliance rate in the covered sector, $e_1 + e_3$, are found in appendix table D.5; the signs of the marginal effects are summarized in the third column of table 5.6.[16] Although most of these effects prove to be not statistically significantly different from zero, perhaps because of the smaller sample sizes involved, it is gratifying to observe that the pattern of effects is quite similar to that which was observed in the complete coverage *CPS* sample.[17] In particular, the noncompliance rate in the partial coverage sample is higher for males than females and for nonwhites than whites, is lower for union members than nonunion members, and declines with an individual's earnings and education level and with the level of resources that the government devotes to compliance activity. As table 5.6 indicates, each of these relationships was also observed in the complete coverage sample.

Conclusions

The evidence presented in this chapter suggests that noncompliance with the overtime pay provisions of the FLSA is a nontrivial problem. The analyses of the May 1978 *CPS* data indicated that at least 9.6 percent of the individuals who worked more than forty-one hours in the survey week and who were believed to be subject to the FLSA's overtime provisions with certainty failed to receive any premium pay for overtime hours. Moreover, from the analyses of the partial coverage *CPS* sample, it can be inferred that over 20 percent of the people working overtime who *were* subject to the overtime pay provisions in those industries in which size-class exemptions existed, failed to receive any premium. Finally, the analyses of the 1977 *QES* data indicated that almost 16 percent of the individuals who worked overtime and who were believed with certainty to be covered by the overtime provisions failed to receive a premium of time and a half.

16. See footnote 7 for an explanation of why the linear probability function model is used rather than the probit model that was used with the complete coverage data.

17. Recall that the analyses of noncompliance in the complete coverage sample were based on 3,231 observations, while the analyses in the partial coverage sample were based on 535 observations.

Together these analyses strongly suggest that 10 percent would be a highly conservative estimate of the noncompliance rate; such a noncompliance rate would substantially moderate the employment effects of an increase in the overtime premium.

These analyses also provide some support for the view that employers' decisions about whether to comply with the overtime pay provisions of the FLSA are at least partially based on the benefits and costs that they believe are associated with noncompliance. To the extent that increasing the overtime premium would increase the benefits employers perceive from noncompliance, this might lead to an increase in noncompliance. If this occurs, the employment effects of an increase in the premium would be further moderated. The analyses in this chapter, however, shed no light on whether this would occur.

TABLE 5.1
Estimates of Violations of
Overtime Provisions of the FLSA, 1965

Category	Establishments in Violation as Percentage of Establishments in which Overtime Was Worked	Percentage of Employees Working Overtime Who Were Not Paid in Accordance with Overtime Provisions
All industries	30%	5.9%
Manufacturing	26	3.6
Food and tobacco	37	8.1
Textiles, apparel and leather	24	3.3
Lumber and furniture	30	3.6
Paper, printing and publishing	25	3.6
Chemicals, petroleum and rubber	27	9.6
Stone, clay, and glass	27	4.4
Metals and metal products	22	1.7
Miscellaneous manufacturing	19	3.1
Nonmanufacturing	32	9.8
Mining	26	7.0
Construction	29	8.2
Transportation, communications, utilities	17	4.5
Wholesale trade—food and farm products	37	11.7
Wholesale trade, all other	40	15.2
Retail trade	47	10.8
Finance and insurance	27	11.7
Real estate	37	39.2
Business service	29	8.9
Other industries	46	10.7
All regions	30	5.9
Northeast	22	3.3
South	37	9.5
Middle West	29	4.3
West	30	7.6
All Sizes of Establishments	30	5.9
Fewer than 10 employees	31	24.9
10–19 employees	38	10.9
20–49 employees	33	11.1
50–99 employees	28	4.7
100 or more employees	25	2.6

Source: Authors' calculations from U.S., Department of Labor, Wage and Hour and Public Contracts Division 1966, tables 9, 10, 11, 17 and 18.

TABLE 5.2

Coverage under the
Overtime Provisions of the FLSA:
Sample Sizes in the May 1978 *CPS*

Category	Number
1. Sample: All those working more than 41 hours during the survey week.	11,738
2. Subsample definitely subject to the overtime pay provisions of the FLSA. (Those paid by the hour).	4,331 (3,231)
3. Subsample subject to the overtime pay provisions of the FLSA with probability that can be calculated. (Those paid by the hour).	944 (535)
4. Subsample not subject to the provisions or coverage cannot be determined.	6,463

Source: May 1978 *CPS*.

TABLE 5.3

Noncompliance with the
Overtime Provisions of the FLSA:
Complete Coverage Sample
(sample sizes in parentheses)

Definition of Noncompliance Represented in Sample	May 1978 CPS		1977 QES
	Private and Federal Employees	Private Employees Only	Private Employees Only
1. Failure to receive *any* premium pay for overtime	23.3% (4,331)	22.8% (4,045)	
2. Failure to receive *any* premium pay for overtime (hourly wage sample)	9.6 (3,231)	8.9 (3,046)	
3. Failure to receive *any* premium pay for overtime (hourly wage sample for which overtime premium can be computed)	9.6 (1,424)	9.2 (1,385)	
4. Failure to receive a premium of at least 1.5 straight-time wage (hourly wage sample for which overtime premium can be computed)	73.3 (1,424)	72.8 (1,385)	15.9% (69)
5. Failure to receive a premium of at least 1.4 straight-time wage (hourly wage sample for which overtime premium can be computed)	64.8 (1,424)	64.3 (1,385)	14.5 (69)

Source: Authors' calculations from the May 1978 *CPS* and from the *1977 Michigan Quality of Employment Survey* data tapes, cited in table sources hereinafter as *QES*.

TABLE 5.4

Proportion of Employees
Covered by the Overtime Provisions,
Selected Retail Trade and Service Industries, 1978

Industry	Coverage Rate
Lumber and building material retailing	.886
Hardware and farm equipment stores	.701
Department and mail order establishments	1.000
Limited price variety stores	.872
Miscellaneous general merchandise stores	.870
Grocery stores	.922
Dairy products stores	.474
Retail bakeries	.324
Food stores, n.e.c.	.587
Motor vehicle dealers	.981
Tire, battery, and accessory dealers	.764
Gasoline service stations	.784
Miscellaneous vehicle dealers	.826
Apparel and accessories stores, except shoe stores	.731
Shoe stores	.540
Furniture and home furnishings stores	.750
Household appliances, TV, and radio stores	.692
Eating and drinking places	.666
Drug stores	.815
Liquor stores	.717
Farm and garden supply stores	.887
Fuel and ice dealers	.882
Retail florists	.285
Miscellaneous retail stores	.527
Automobile services, except repair	.719
Automobile repair and related services	.607
Electrical repair shops	.607
Miscellaneous repair services	.511
Hotels and motels	.881
Beauty shops	.084
Barber shops	.040
Shoe repair shops	.059
Dressmaking shops	.565
Miscellaneous personal services	.686
Bowling alleys, billiard and pool parlors	.631
Miscellaneous entertainment and recreation services	.717

Source: Authors' calculations from unpublished tabulations prepared by the U.S. Bureau of the Census from data from the *1977 Census of Retail Trade* and *1977 Census of Selected Service Industries.*

TABLE 5.5

Noncompliance with the
Overtime Provisions of the FLSA:
Partial Coverage Sample, 1978

Model	Covered Sector (P_c)	Noncovered Sector (P_n)
1. Noncompliance constant within each sector	20.2%	64.2%
2. Noncompliance varies within each sector with characteristics of the individual	24.5	48.5
3. Noncompliance constant within the noncovered sector, varies in the covered sector with the industry coverage ratio	49.0	−1.3
4. Noncompliance varies within each sector with characteristics of the individual and in the covered sector with the industry coverage ratio	59.7	−33.4

Source: Authors' calculations using regression results based on the May 1978 CPS. Regression results found in appendix tables D.2 and D.3, columns (1) and (4).

TABLE 5.6

Determinants of Noncompliance:
Summary of Hypotheses and Results

Variable	Hypothesized Effect	Estimated Effects		
		Probit Results, Complete Coverage, CPS Sample[a]	Probit Results, Complete Coverage, QES Sample[b]	OLS Results, Partial Coverage, CPS Sample[a]
Age	− then +	+*	+	−
Sex (1 = male; 0 = female)	?	+	+	+
Race (1 = nonwhite; 0 = white)	?	+	+*	+
Hispanic (1 = yes; 0 = no)	+	0		+
Education	−	−	+	−
Earnings level	−	−*	0	−*
Union status	−	−*	−*	−
Concentrated industries	−	−*	−	
Government resources devoted to compliance	−	−		−

Notes: Results summarized from appendix tables D.1, D.2, and D.3.

All samples restricted to hourly wage workers.

[a] Noncompliance defined as failure to receive any premium.

[b] Noncompliance defined as failure to receive a premium of at least time and a half.

+(−) Increase in the variable increases (decreases) noncompliance.

* Estimated coefficient was statistically significantly different from zero at the .05 level of significance.

6· THE INCOME DISTRIBUTION EFFECTS OF THE OVERTIME PAY PROVISIONS OF THE FLSA

Research on the overtime pay provisions of the FLSA, including the new research reported in the previous chapters, has concentrated on the effects of the legislation on hours of work and employment. Surprisingly, no attention has been directed to the income distribution consequences of the existence of overtime hours, the current hours legislation, or proposals that would alter the legislation.[1] Virtually nothing is known about how compensation for overtime hours influences the distribution of family incomes or about how changing the overtime premium would alter this distribution. Since policy makers should be concerned with the income distribution consequences of legislation as well as their efficiency effects, the answers to these questions are of utmost importance.

The analyses of the May 1978 *Current Population Survey* data that follow attempt to answer these questions. Although the analyses are subject to numerous qualifications, they suggest that both the current legislation and proposals that would raise the overtime premium to double time yield greater benefits to middle and upper

---

1. Two researchers have previously looked at the income distributional consequences of minimum wage legislation. Gramlich (1976) examined the distribution of low-wage workers by family income class, and Kelly (1976) simulated the effect of an increase in the minimum wage on the number of families below the poverty line, assuming that the minimum wage had no disemployment effects. More generally, a procedure for evaluating the social benefits of income redistribution programs has been proposed in Gramlich and Wolkoff (1979).

income families than they do to lower income families. In this sense, the overtime pay provisions of the FLSA are regressive in nature.

The Data and Their Limitations

Although the *CPS* appears to be the best data set available for investigating the question of income distribution effects of the overtime pay provisions of the FLSA, there are a number of reasons the data contained in each May's survey are not ideal for calculating the effects of the overtime pay premium, or changes in the premium, on the distribution of family incomes. First, the units of observation in the *CPS* are individuals, not families, although it is possible to identify members of the same family. The *CPS* sample is a stratified random sample, not a complete census, and in building up to the population totals on overtime income per family from the *CPS* sample, each *CPS* observation must be weighted by its sampling weight. But, since all members of a family do not necessarily receive the same sample weight, it is difficult to derive totals for family units. In the calculations that follow, this problem is circumvented by assuming that no more than one individual works overtime in any family unit. This assumption appears to be fairly reasonable, and since family income is reported separately for each individual in the sample, this eliminates the need to construct family units from the *CPS* data, that is, the assumption permits the estimation of average overtime earnings in each family income class directly from the data on individuals.[2]

Second, the *CPS* contains information on the number of overtime hours, defined as hours in excess of forty worked during the survey week and, for individuals who worked overtime, their usual weekly hours. But no information is reported on total weeks worked during the year. This forces the assumption that individuals working overtime are all employed for the full year. This is clearly an errone-

---

2. This assumption will not alter the following conclusions substantially. If more than one individual in a family works overtime, it will cause an overstatement of the proportion of families in each income class in which overtime is worked and an understatement of average overtime earnings of those families in which overtime is worked. But average overtime earnings in each family income class, the product of the two variables, will be unchanged.

ous assumption for individuals from families with low annual family incomes and, as will be obvious below, causes an overstatement of the contribution of overtime hours to their annual incomes.

Third, data are reported on whether an overtime pay premium was received for overtime hours, but not on the rate of the premium. While it is possible to compute an estimate of the overtime premium for a subsample of observations, this computation is fraught with errors and leads to estimates of noncompliance that are as high as 73 percent (see in Chapter 5 the section on new estimates of noncompliance). In light of this, it is assumed for purposes of the simulations that follow that all individuals who report receiving an overtime premium received a premium of time and a half. Each of these assumptions introduces some error into the simulations, which suggests that the results must be considered only tentative.

Preliminary Information

The May 1978 *CPS* contains data for each individual on the annual family income of the household in which the individual resided and on whether the individual is the "principal person" (head of household) in the family. Summing those individuals who were principal persons and weighting each observation by its sampling weight, one finds that the May 1978 *CPS* represented about 76.5 million households, of which 8.0 percent failed to report their family income (table 6.1). The analyses in this chapter focus on those families that reported their family incomes.

If it is assumed that no more than one individual in each family worked overtime during the survey week, it is possible to calculate the number of families in which overtime hours were worked during the survey week. These numbers are tabulated in table 6.1 for four different samples used in the analyses. The first represents those families for which survey week hours exceeded forty; there are 17.2 million families in this sample. The second is those families for which survey week hours and usual weekly hours were greater than forty; this sample includes roughly 11.9 million families. The third sample includes those families for which survey week hours were greater than forty and premium pay was received, some 7.3 million families. The fourth accounts for those families for which survey week hours and usual weekly hours exceeded forty and premium pay was received, a sample of 3.7 million households.

These figures imply that during the survey week, while 22.5 percent of all families contained an individual who worked more than forty hours, only 9.5 percent of the families contained an individual who received premium pay for overtime. Moreover, if the sample is restricted to those families in which overtime was worked both during the survey week and usually, these percentages fall to 15.5 and 4.9, respectively.

This raises the question of whether the analyses of the income distributional effects of the overtime premium should be restricted to families in which a family member *usually* worked more than forty hours. On the one hand, imposing the restriction would understate the contribution of overtime hours to total family income because it would ignore the overtime earnings both of people who worked overtime during the survey week but did not usually work overtime and of people who usually worked overtime but did not work overtime during the survey week.[3] On the other hand, failure to impose the restriction would overstate the overtime income earned by those individuals who worked overtime during the survey week but did not usually work overtime, since the simulations that follow assume that the number of overtime hours worked during the survey week are also worked each week. Since imposing the restriction understates overtime earnings, while failure to impose it overstates overtime earnings, it seems prudent to conduct analyses for both cases.

The last column of table 6.1 presents data on the percentage of individuals in each sample that did not report their annual family incomes. The fraction ranges from 5.2 percent for all those who reported working overtime to 3.0 to 3.5 percent for those who received premium pay for overtime. While these fractions are smaller than the 8.0 percent of the overall population that failed to report total family income, they are still significant. While one could attempt to devise an algorithm to impute total family income to nonreporters, the analysis that follows simply omits such individuals.

3. Information on receipt of premium pay for overtime hours is available in the *CPS* only for those individuals who reported working overtime during the survey week.

Table 6.2 presents the first information relevant to the question of the income distribution consequences of the overtime pay premium and overtime hours. For the subsample of families who reported their total incomes, it presents, for each of the four overtime samples, tabulations of the distribution of total family income in the population and the distributions of those working overtime by total family income class.

These data indicate quite clearly that the distribution of those working overtime, by family income class, is weighted more heavily toward the upper levels of the income distribution than is the overall distribution of individuals reporting family income. For example, the fraction of individuals in each family income class up to the $10,000 level is substantially larger than the fraction of individuals who work overtime that are members of those family income classes. As a result, while 39.6 percent of all families reported total family incomes of less than $10,000, only 15 to 18 percent (depending upon the definition of overtime used) of individuals who worked overtime came from families with family incomes below this level. A similar divergence occurs if the cutoff is made at $15,000; indeed, while 25.6 percent of all families reported family incomes of greater than $20,000 in May 1978, 34.4 to 45. 9 percent of the individuals working overtime came from these income classes.

Another way of conveying the same information is to focus on the percentage of households in each family income class in which some family member works overtime. These tabulations are presented in table 6.3; they indicate that the percentages are substantially higher in the upper income levels. Indeed, regardless of the definition of overtime used, the percentage increases monotonically with family income over the $2,000 to $25,000 range;[4] that is, the probability that a family has a member working overtime increases with family income.

Of course, these data refer to the probability of working over-

---

4. It continues to increase in the range above $25,000 if overtime is not defined to require receipt of a premium. If receipt of premium pay is required, the percentage declines in the upper income levels, reflecting the fact that many of these individuals are self-employed or exempt from the overtime pay provisions of the FLSA.

time; they provide no information on how average weekly overtime hours for those individuals working overtime varies with family income. If individuals from low-income families who work overtime systematically have longer workweeks than individuals from high-income families who work overtime, it is possible that the distribution of overtime hours across family income classes may actually be more heavily weighted toward the lower income classes. Put another way, average overtime hours per family may not increase with family income levels.

In fact, the data tabulated in table 6.4 suggest that average weekly overtime hours for those individuals working overtime are not substantially higher for individuals from lower income families than for those from upper income families.[5] As such, the conclusion that average overtime hours per family, the probability of working overtime (table 6.3) multiplied by average overtime hours if they are worked (table 6.4), are higher for higher income families than they are for lower income families is also true. This conclusion appears to hold regardless of whether the definition of overtime requires receipt of premium pay.

The next task is to compute average *annual* overtime earnings per person for those individuals who work overtime. To do so requires a number of assumptions: that each employee works fifty weeks per year; that the overtime premium is time and a half for all those who report receiving premium pay for overtime; that average weekly overtime hours equal an individual's survey week overtime hours; and that the premium goes into effect after forty hours a week for all workers.[6] Furthermore, it is assumed that those individuals who failed to report their usual weekly earnings, a variable needed to calculate their straight-time and overtime hourly wage

---

5. Weekly overtime hours are defined here as the difference between usual weekly hours and forty.

6. Privately negotiated collective bargaining agreements often call for premium pay to go into effect before forty hours; however, the *CPS* data do not permit us to identify individuals who might be subject to such provisions. Survey week overtime hours are used in this calculation since for individuals who did not usually work overtime (table 6.5), usual overtime hours as defined in footnote 5 would be negative. As discussed earlier, these individuals are included in the computations to control for the omission of individuals who did not work overtime during the particular survey week but did work overtime in other weeks.

rates, earn the mean value of usual weekly earnings reported by individuals in the same family income classes as they.

With these assumptions, the calculations of average annual overtime earnings for those individuals working overtime, by family income class, are straightforward; these calculations are presented in table 6.5. When the samples are restricted to those who receive premium pay for overtime, these numbers are simply the average across individuals working overtime, weighted by the sample weights, of estimated annual overtime hours multiplied by one and one half their straight-time wage rate. When the samples are not restricted to those receiving premium pay, both premium pay for overtime and straight-time pay for overtime are included in the computations.

The answers that such calculations yield for the low income groups clearly are not correct. For example, for family incomes of less than $3,000, the calculations often show that average annual overtime earnings for those working overtime exceeds the total family income that the individual reported. Individuals with family incomes of less than $3,000 could not have worked overtime for fifty weeks; this assumption probably has led to a systematic overstatement of the annual overtime income of those individuals from low-income families who worked overtime, which suggests that the simulations of policy change that follow systematically overstate the overtime earnings of individuals from low-income families. Overtime earnings are likely to be more regressively distributed than the results indicate. Nevertheless, it is interesting to note that after the $3,000 level, annual overtime earnings per individual working overtime does increase monotonically with family income class.

Simulations of Policy Changes

The data presented in the preceding tables can be used to simulate, by income class, the changes in average annual family income that would result from various changes in overtime hours and the overtime premium. Initial estimates are presented in table 6.6 where the sample is restricted to those individuals whose survey week hours and usual weekly hours exceed forty, and in table 6.7, where all individuals who worked more than forty hours during the survey week are included.

First, what would be the effect on average annual family income of eliminating all premium pay for overtime, while holding constant overtime hours? This reduction is equivalent to the average annual premium pay for overtime per family that is currently received and is computed by multiplying the fraction of families that contain an individual working overtime for premium pay (table 6.3) by the premium pay for overtime that an individual working overtime received (table 6.5).

The answers, reported in the first column of tables 6.6 and 6.7, suggest that premium pay for overtime currently contributes very little to average annual family incomes of low-income families. Indeed, according to these estimates, families with annual incomes of less than $4,000 in 1978 averaged less than $10 apiece in premium pay for overtime, primarily because less than 2 percent of these families had a family member who worked overtime for premium pay (table 6.3). In contrast, families with family incomes in the $20,000 to $49,999 range received premium pay for overtime in excess of $130 per year, on average.

Next, what would be the effect of eliminating all overtime hours, both with and without premium pay? This is equivalent to asking what the effect on annual family income of working hours in excess of forty per week is. The answers are obtained by multiplying the annual overtime income per person (table 6.5) by the percentage of families in an income class in which an individual worked overtime (table 6.3), and these are tabulated in the second columns of tables 6.6 and 6.7.

Overtime earnings per family are seen to increase substantially with family income class, rising from under $100 per family in the lowest family income classes to over $2,300 per family in the highest income class. This occurs because the probability of working long hours increases substantially with family income, as does annual overtime earnings of those individuals working overtime. The reader should be cautioned, however, that these overtime earnings figures include the earnings of the self-employed and of professionals and others who are exempt from the overtime pay provisions of the FLSA. Legislating prohibitions against long workweeks for employees covered by the legislation would have no where near as drastic effects as these results might suggest. Indeed, such effects would at most equal three times those found in the first columns of tables 6.6 and 6.7.[7]

Suppose next that the overtime premium was raised to double time and that hours of work and employment were held constant. In this case, average annual overtime earnings would increase in each income class; the increase would be equal to the average annual premium pay per family currently received from overtime work. These numbers are tabulated in the third column of tables 6.6 and 6.7. They increase substantially with family income up to $50,000, suggesting that upper income level families would gain more from the increase in the premium than would lower income families.

Of course, such a calculation is not very useful since it precludes the very phenomenon that an increase in the premium is supposed to induce, a reduction in overtime hours and an increase in employment. Prior estimates of the effect of raising the overtime premium to double time, and those reported in Chapter 2, suggest that at most a 10 to 40 percent reduction in overtime hours would occur, with 20 percent probably being a best estimate. Such overtime reductions are built into the simulations in the last four columns of tables 6.6 and 6.7, still maintaining the assumption of no resulting employment gains, however.

Including the reduction in overtime hours in the simulations reduces the magnitudes of the resulting earnings gains but leaves them positive, for reductions of less than 40 percent.[8] Upper income families continue to gain more than lower income families. With a 30 percent reduction in overtime hours, however, annual earnings per family would increase by less than $10 for virtually all classes. If overtime hours were reduced by 40 percent, a highly unlikely result, annual earnings would decline for each family income class and the decline would be larger, in absolute terms, for higher income groups. Families in the $20,000 to $49,999 range would see their average incomes fall by around $28, a decline of roughly 0.1 percent.

To complete the evaluation of the income distributional consequences of raising the overtime premium to double time, it is

---

7. Some individuals who receive premium pay for overtime may not be covered by the overtime pay provisions of the FLSA and compliance with a provision banning all long work weeks would not be complete.

8. More precisely, for reductions of less than 33.33 percent.

necessary to know the number of new jobs created and the distribution of these jobs across family income classes. Suppose initially that all the reduction in overtime is converted to new full-time jobs (fifty weeks at forty hours a week), each of which pays the mean hourly wage of employed individuals in the family income class that the unemployed individual is coming from. Suppose also that the jobs are distributed across family income classes in proportion to the percent of all experienced unemployed in the family income class; these percentages are tabulated in table 6.8 and imply, for example, that 11.42 percent of the new jobs would go to unemployed individuals from families with incomes in the $7,500 to $9,999 range.

With these assumptions, it is possible to compute the increases in annual family income, by income class, that would result from the increased employment associated with the increase in the overtime premium to double time. These numbers are tabulated in table 6.9 for the various percentage reductions in overtime hours. They suggest family income gains due to the employment increase that are in the range of $10 to $50, depending upon the assumed reduction in overtime hours. Furthermore, there is no significant variation in income gain across family income classes. Although the probability of obtaining one of these new jobs declines as family income increases (table 6.8, second column), the average wage of employed individuals in the family income class appears to vary in a compensating manner (table 6.8, third column).

The net effect of raising the overtime premium on the distribution of family incomes can be summarized by adding together the estimates found in tables 6.8 and 6.9. This is done in table 6.10 for the cases in which the sample is restricted to those individuals who usually work more than forty hours; the results for all individuals who worked more than forty hours during the survey week are virtually identical. For changes in overtime hours of 10 and 20 percent, the net effect on the distribution of family income is regressive, in the sense that average family income gains tend to increase with family income. With a 30 percent reduction in overtime, the gain in average family income is roughly the same across income classes. Only if raising the overtime premium to double time caused a reduction in overtime hours of 40 percent would lower income families gain more, on average, than higher income families. Previous studies and the present one suggest that a reduction in overtime of such a magnitude is highly unlikely.

It is also unlikely, as argued in Chapters 3 through 5, that all the reduction in overtime would be converted to new full-time jobs or that the new jobs would be distributed among family income classes in proportion to their share of the experienced unemployed. Such an assignment procedure ignores the fact that the occupational distributions of those working overtime and the experienced unemployed associated with each family income class may differ widely. For example, if experienced unemployed workers from low-income families are overrepresented in occupations in which little overtime is worked, they will get less than their proportionate share of the newly created jobs; and this will increase the regressive nature of an increase in the overtime premium.

The final sets of simulations relax the assumptions about the number of jobs created and how these jobs are allocated. Suppose first that only one-half the reduction in overtime was converted to new full-time jobs, a fraction that the analyses in Chapters 3 through 5 suggest is likely to be an optimistic estimate. Table 6.11 contrasts the average family income gains associated with a 20 percent reduction in overtime for this rate of conversion with conversion of all the reduction in overtime to new full-time jobs. While the magnitudes of all of the income gains decline in this case, the conclusion that higher income families would gain more than lower income families continues to hold.

Next, suppose that rather than the new jobs being assigned to family income classes in proportion to their share of the experienced unemployed in each class, the fact that the occupational distribution of the experienced unemployed varies across family income classes is accounted for. Specifically, suppose that the new jobs created in each occupation class are distributed across family income classes in proportion to the fraction of the experienced unemployed in the occupation that are members of each family income class. The results of these simulations, similar to those described above save for this one assumption, are reported in the last two columns of table 6.11.

Somewhat surprisingly, these results differ only marginally from the previous ones. The earnings gains in the lower income classes (under $6,000) diminish slightly, those in the $6,000 to

$15,000 range increase slightly; and the only fairly substantial change is in the $15,000 to $19,999 range, where a drop occurs. As table 6.12 indicates, this probably occurs because the unemployed in this group are proportionately underrepresented in the operative category in which substantial overtime is worked. While 25 percent of all those working overtime were operatives, as were over 20 percent of the experienced unemployed from families with incomes of less than $15,000, only 16 percent of the experienced unemployed from families with incomes in the $15,000 to $19,999 range fell in this category. In general, however, the occupational distribution of the experienced unemployed does not differ across family income classes sufficiently to substantially alter the conclusions about the income distribution consequences of an increase in the overtime premium.

Conclusions

This chapter has presented the first analyses of how compensation for overtime hours influences the distribution of family incomes and how changing the overtime premium would alter this distribution. Although these results are subject to numerous qualifications, they suggest that both the current legislation and proposals that would raise the overtime premium to double time yield greater benefits to middle income and upper income families than they do to lower income families. In this sense, the overtime pay provisions of the FLSA are regressive in nature.

   In large part, these conclusions result from the fact that the probability that an individual will be working overtime increases with his or her family income class, as does annual overtime earnings per family over a wide range. Unless an increase in the overtime premium to double time induced more than a 33 percent decline in the usage of overtime, a decline that the results in Chapters 3 through 5 suggest is unlikely, average overtime income would actually increase for each income class. Furthermore, the distribution of the experienced unemployed is not sufficiently skewed towards individuals from low-income families to assure that such individuals would get the lion's share of the new jobs that potentially might be created from the reduction in overtime hours. As such, on balance it appears that an increase in the overtime premium to double time would increase the average incomes of middle income and upper income families by more than it would the average incomes of lower income families.

TABLE 6.1

Samples Used in the Simulations

Sample	Number	Number Not Reporting Family Income	Percentage Not Reporting Family Income
Total families	76,521,361	6,086,199	8.0%
Families with member working overtime			
Survey week hours > 40	17,229,044	854,117	5.0
Survey week and usual weekly hours > 40	11,868,058	620,624	5.2
Survey week hours > 40, receipt of premium pay	7,288,514	234,773	3.2
Survey week and usual weekly hours > 40, receipt of premium pay	3,743,779	131,253	3.5

Source: Authors' calculations from the May 1978 *CPS*.

TABLE 6.2

Distribution of Family Incomes
and Those Working Overtime,
1978

Family Income Class	Percentage of Families	Workers Reporting Survey Week Hours		Workers Reporting Usual Weekly and Survey Week Hours	
		>40	>40, Received Premium Pay	>40	>40, Received Premium Pay
Less than $1,000	1.3%	0.4%	0.2%	0.5%	0.2%
$1,000–1,999	1.9	0.4	0.3	0.3	0.3
$2,000–2,999	4.7	0.7	0.8	0.6	0.6
$3,000–3,999	5.5	0.9	0.9	0.9	0.9
$4,000–4,999	4.9	1.4	1.4	1.3	1.2
$5,000–5,999	5.1	2.0	2.2	2.1	2.3
$6,000–7,499	6.6	3.3	3.6	3.2	3.6
$7,500–9,999	9.6	6.7	8.4	6.2	8.3
Less than $10,000	39.6	15.8	18.0	15.1	17.4
$10,000–11,999	8.4	7.7	9.3	7.5	9.8
$12,000–14,999	11.5	12.9	16.1	12.3	16.3
Less than 15,000	59.5	36.4	43.4	34.9	43.5
$15,000–19,999	14.9	20.3	22.5	19.2	20.5
$20,000–24,999	11.3	17.4	17.6	17.1	17.6
$25,000–49,999	12.4	22.1	16.1	24.2	17.5
$50,000 or more	1.9	3.5	0.7	4.6	0.9

Source: Authors' calculations from the May 1978 *CPS*.

TABLE 6.3

Percentage of Households with
Some Family Member Working Overtime,
1978

Family Income Class	Workers Reporting Survey Week Hours		Workers Reporting Survey Week and Usual Weekly Hours	
	>40	>40, Received Premium Pay	>40	>40, Received Premium Pay
Less than $1,000	7.2%	1.3%	6.5%	0.9%
$1,000–1,999	4.4	1.8	2.8	0.7
$2,000–2,999	3.6	1.6	2.1	0.6
$3,000–3,999	3.8	1.6	2.5	0.9
$4,000–4,999	6.7	2.9	4.3	1.2
$5,000–5,999	9.4	4.3	6.6	2.3
$6,000–7,499	11.6	5.4	7.7	2.8
$7,500–9,999	16.1	8.8	10.3	4.4
$10,000–11,999	21.5	11.0	14.2	6.0
$12,000–14,999	26.1	14.0	17.0	7.3
$15,000–19,999	31.7	15.1	20.6	7.1
$20,000–24,999	35.9	15.6	24.1	8.0
$25,000–49,999	41.4	12.9	31.1	7.2
$50,000 or more	44.5	3.8	39.2	2.3

Source: Authors' calculations from the May 1978 *CPS*.

TABLE 6.4

Average Weekly Overtime Hours for
Individuals Working Overtime

Family Income Class	Workers Working Overtime	Workers Working Overtime, Receiving Premium Pay
Less than $1,000	16.8	7.6
$1,000–1,999	9.6	7.5
$2,000–2,999	16.4	14.6
$3,000–3,999	14.5	10.4
$4,000–4,999	13.4	9.8
$5,000–5,999	13.5	10.2
$6,000–7,499	12.7	9.7
$7,500–9,999	12.7	9.3
$10,000–11,999	11.7	9.5
$12,000–14,999	11.8	9.3
$15,000–19,999	12.0	9.4
$20,000–24,999	12.1	10.7
$25,000–49,999	11.9	10.4
$50,000 or more	15.0	14.6

Source: Authors' calculations from the May 1978 *CPS*.

Note: Overtime is defined as survey week and usual weekly hours being greater than 40.

TABLE 6.5

Average Annual Overtime Income
for Individuals Working Overtime

Family Income Class	Workers Reporting Survey Week Hours		Workers Reporting Survey Week and Usual Weekly Hours	
	>40	>40, Received Premium Pay	>40	>40, Received Premium Pay
Less than $1,000	$1,511	$1,389	$1,673	$1,888
$1,000–1,999	1,168	613	1,895	1,591
$2,000–2,999	1,882	1,848	3,217	4,934
$3,000–3,999	1,397	1,210	2,198	2,511
$4,000–4,999	1,308	1,128	2,128	2,622
$5,000–5,999	1,615	1,157	2,619	2,623
$6,000–7,499	1,564	1,508	2,444	3,051
$7,500–9,999	1,643	1,472	2,722	3,001
$10,000–11,999	1,891	1,713	2,993	3,176
$12,000–14,999	2,090	1,925	3,195	3,394
$15,000–19,999	2,165	1,536	3,758	4,071
$20,000–24,999	2,807	2,601	4,394	5,041
$25,000–49,999	3,651	3,045	5,123	5,476
$50,000 or more	5,380	4,072	6,294	6,580

Source: Authors' calculations from the May 1978 *CPS*.

TABLE 6.6
Changes in Average Annual Family Income from
Various Changes in Overtime Hours and the Overtime Premium:
Individuals Whose Usual Weekly Hours Exceed 40

Family Income Class	Reduction in Earnings			Increase in Earnings from Raising Premium to Double Time and Reduction in Overtime, No New Employment			
	No Premium, Overtime Constant	Elimination of all Overtime	Premium Raised to Double Time, Overtime Constant	10% Reduction	20% Reduction	30% Reduction	40% Reduction
Less than $1,000	$5.88	$108.48	-$5.88	$4.05	$2.29	$0.53	-$1.23
$1,000–1,999	3.66	52.38	-3.66	2.53	1.43	0.33	-0.77
$2,000–2,999	9.97	68.51	-9.97	6.88	3.89	0.90	-2.09
$3,000–3,999	7.22	55.48	-7.22	4.98	2.82	0.65	-1.52
$4,000–4,999	10.86	92.41	-10.86	7.49	4.24	0.98	-2.28
$5,000–5,999	20.34	173.22	-20.34	14.03	7.93	1.83	-4.27
$6,000–7,499	28.53	188.32	-28.53	19.68	11.13	2.57	-5.99
$7,500–9,999	44.01	280.17	-44.01	30.37	17.16	3.96	-9.24
$10,000–11,999	63.68	426.14	-63.68	43.94	24.84	5.73	-13.37
$12,000–14,999	82.17	545.30	-82.17	56.69	32.04	7.39	-17.26
$15,000–19,999	95.99	772.52	-95.99	66.23	37.44	8.64	-20.16
$20,000–24,999	134.36	1061.65	-134.36	92.71	52.40	12.09	-28.22
$25,000–49,999	132.12	1594.10	-132.13	91.17	51.53	11.89	-27.75
$50,000 or more	52.19	2469.01	-52.19	36.01	20.35	4.70	-10.96

Source: Authors' calculations from the May 1978 CPS.

TABLE 6.7
Changes in Average Annual Family Income from Various Changes in Overtime Hours and the Overtime Premium: Individuals Whose Survey Week Hours Exceed 40

Family Income Class	Reduction in Earnings			Increase in Earnings from Raising Premium to Double Time, Reduction in Overtime, No New Employment			
	No Premium, Overtime Constant	Elimination of all Overtime	Premium Raised to Double Time, Overtime Constant	10% Reduction	20% Reduction	30% Reduction	40% Reduction
Less than $1,000	$5.88	$108.48	−$5.88	$4.05	$2.29	$0.53	−$1.23
$1,000–1,999	3.66	51.74	−3.66	2.53	1.43	0.33	−0.77
$2,000–2,999	9.78	67.94	−9.78	6.75	3.81	0.88	−2.05
$3,000–3,999	6.65	53.12	−6.65	4.59	2.59	0.60	−1.40
$4,000–4,999	10.76	88.01	−10.76	7.42	4.19	0.97	−2.26
$5,000–5,999	16.64	151.17	−16.64	11.48	6.49	1.50	−3.50
$6,000–7,499	27.19	180.83	−27.19	18.76	18.60	2.45	−5.71
$7,500–9,999	42.95	265.00	−42.95	29.63	16.75	3.87	−9.02
$10,000–11,999	63.12	407.39	−63.12	43.55	24.62	5.68	−13.26
$12,000–14,999	89.99	546.49	−89.99	62.09	35.10	8.10	−18.90
$15,000–19,999	77.52	687.71	−77.52	53.49	30.23	6.98	−16.28
$20,000–24,999	135.43	1007.34	−135.43	93.45	52.82	12.19	−28.44
$25,000–49,999	131.37	1511.49	−131.37	90.64	51.23	11.82	−27.59
$50,000 or more	52.19	2396.77	−52.19	36.01	20.35	4.70	−10.96

Source: Authors' calculations from the May 1978 CPS.

TABLE 6.8

Distribution of the Experienced
Unemployed and Average Wage

Family Income Class	Number of Experienced Unemployed	Percent of All Experienced Unemployed	Percent of Families with an Experienced Unemployed Individual	Average Wage of Employeed Individuals
Less than $1,000	94,961	2.10%	10.6%	$3.20
$1,000–1,999	146,958	3.25	10.9	3.07
$2,000–2,999	196,726	4.35	5.9	4.11
$3,000–3,999	228,555	5.06	5.9	3.15
$4,000–4,999	298,896	6.62	8.6	3.58
$5,000–5,999	308,970	6.84	8.7	3.68
$6,000–7,499	354,273	7.84	7.6	4.05
$7,500–9,999	515,660	11.42	7.6	4.24
$10,000–11,999	387,589	8.58	6.6	4.62
$12,000–14,999	483,723	10.71	6.0	4.97
$15,000–19,999	567,513	12.56	5.4	5.86
$20,000–24,999	421,673	9.33	5.3	6.52
$25,000–49,999	447,228	9.90	5.1	7.01
$50,000 or more	62,299	1.38	4.7	5.69

Source: Authors' calculations from the May 1978 *CPS*.

TABLE 6.9

Increases in Average Annual Family Income
Due to the New Jobs Created if
a Fraction of All Overtime Worked at Premium Pay Were Eliminated
and Redistributed in the Form of New Full-Time Jobs

Family Income Class	Overtime Defined as Survey Week and Usual Weekly Hours > 40				Overtime Defined as Survey Week Hours > 40			
	10% Reduction	20% Reduction	30% Reduction	40% Reduction	10% Reduction	20% Reduction	30% Reduction	40% Reduction
Less than $1,000	$13.51	$27.01	$40.52	$54.02	$13.10	$26.19	$39.28	$52.38
$1,000–1,999	13.31	26.61	39.92	53.22	12.90	25.80	38.70	51.61
$2,000–2,999	9.61	19.22	28.83	38.43	9.32	18.63	27.95	37.27
$3,000–3,999	7.35	14.70	22.05	29.40	7.13	14.25	21.38	28.50
$4,000–4,999	12.24	24.48	36.72	48.96	11.87	23.74	35.60	47.47
$5,000–5,999	19.64	25.28	37.92	50.55	12.25	24.51	36.76	49.02
$6,000–7,499	12.25	24.50	36.75	49.00	11.88	23.76	35.63	47.51
$7,500–9,999	12.77	25.53	38.30	51.06	12.38	24.76	37.13	49.51
$10,000–11,999	12.00	24.00	36.00	48.00	11.64	23.27	34.91	46.54
$12,000–14,999	11.76	23.53	35.30	47.06	11.41	22.81	34.22	45.63
$15,000–19,999	12.57	25.14	37.71	50.28	12.19	24.37	36.56	48.75
$20,000–24,999	13.70	27.41	41.11	54.81	13.29	26.57	39.86	53.15
$25,000–49,999	14.20	28.40	42.60	56.80	13.77	27.54	41.31	55.07
$50,000 or more	10.67	21.34	32.01	42.68	10.34	20.69	31.03	41.38

Source: Authors' calculations from the May 1978 *CPS*.

Note: The calculations assume that the new jobs created will be filled by the experienced unemployed. Also, they considered only the income gain due to the new jobs, not the income changes due to the change in the overtime premium and overtime hours.

TABLE 6.10

Change in Average Annual Family Income from
Reduction of All Overtime Worked for Premium Pay
and Redistribution of These Hours
in the Form of New Full-Time Jobs

Family Income Class	10% Reduction	20% Reduction	30% Reduction	40% Reduction
Less than $1,000	$17.56	$29.30	$41.04	$52.79
$1,000–1,999	15.82	28.09	40.25	52.45
$2,000–2,999	16.69	23.10	29.73	36.34
$3,000–3,999	12.33	17.52	22.70	28.88
$4,000–4,999	19.73	28.72	37.10	46.48
$5,000–5,999	24.67	33.21	39.75	46.28
$6,000–7,499	32.53	35.63	38.32	43.01
$7,500–9,999	43.14	43.69	41.26	41.82
$10,000–11,999	55.94	48.84	41.73	34.63
$12,000—14,999	68.45	55.57	42.69	29.80
$15,000–19,999	78.80	65.58	46.35	30.12
$20,000–24,999	106.41	79.81	53.20	26.59
$25,000–49,999	105.37	79.98	54.49	29.05
$50,000 or more	46.68	41.69	36.70	31.72

Source: Authors' calculations from the May 1978 *CPS*.
Notes: Overtime is defined as survey week and usual weekly hours greater than 40.

These calculations assume that new jobs will be filled by the experienced unemployed.

TABLE 6.11

Change in Average Annual Family Income Resulting from
20 Percent Reduction of
All Overtime Worked for Premium Pay
and Redistribution of a Fraction of Those Hours
in the Form of New Full-Time Jobs

Family Income Class	100% Redistribution[a]	50% Redistribution[a]	100% Redistribution by Occupation[b]	50% Redistribution by Occupation[b]
Less than $1,000	$29.30	$15.80	$26.08	$14.19
$1,000–1,999	28.09	14.79	24.06	12.75
$2,000–2,999	23.10	13.50	20.98	12.40
$3,000–3,999	17.52	10.18	15.36	8.98
$4,000–4,999	28.72	16.48	28.70	16.63
$5,000–5,999	33.21	20.57	32.42	19.46
$6,000–7,499	35.63	23.38	35.82	23.21
$7,500–9,999	43.69	30.43	44.72	30.74
$10,000–11,999	48.84	36.53	51.72	38.16
$12,000–14,999	55.57	43.81	58.32	46.71
$15,000–19,999	65.58	53.01	54.97	42.60
$20,000–24,999	79.81	66.10	81.15	66.98
$25,000–49,999	79.98	65.78	77.74	64.48
$50,000 or more	41.69	31.02	40.53	30.44

Source: Authors' calculations from the May 1978 CPS.
Notes: Overtime is defined as survey week and usual weekly hours greater than 40.

[a] Jobs are redistributed across family income classes in proportion to the fraction of experienced unemployed in the income class.

[b] Jobs created in each occupation are distributed across family income classes in proportion to the fraction of experienced unemployed in that occupation in each class.

TABLE 6.12

Those Working Overtime and
the Experienced Unemployed in Each Family Income Class,
by Major Occupational Group

Family Income Class	Professional	Managers	Sales	Clerical	Craftsmen	Operatives
Percent working overtime	8%	4%	2%	14%	27%	25%
<$1,000	3	1	4	11	10	25
$1,000–1,999	5	2	5	13	5	24
$2,000–2,999	2	5	4	11	8	24
$3,000–3,999	2	2	6	14	6	21
$4,000–4,999	6	4	4	11	9	24
$5,000–5,999	5	2	4	17	10	24
$6,000–7,499	5	2	4	20	11	22
$7,500–9,999	5	5	3	16	12	24
$10,000–11,000	6	6	7	15	12	21
$12,000–14,999	5	4	8	22	10	20
$15,999–19,999	10	4	5	25	11	16
$20,000–24,999	9	4	4	22	12	16
$25,000–49,999	11	4	6	21	9	12
$50,000 or more	17	11	12	12	6	15

Family Income Class	Transport Operatives	Laborers	Household	Service	Farmers	Farm Laborers
Percent working overtime	8%	7%	0%	6%	0%	0%
<$1,000	1	10	7	24	0	2
$1,000–1,999	3	8	3	21	0	10
$2,000–2,999	2	11	3	29	0	1
$3,000–3,999	4	13	1	28	1	1
$4,000–4,999	4	10	1	23	0	4
$5,000–5,999	5	13	1	18	0	1
$6,000–7,499	5	12	1	18	0	1
$7,500–9,999	5	9	0	19	0	2
$10,000–11,000	6	10	0	16	0	2
$12,000–14,999	4	8	0	16	0	2
$15,999–19,999	3	8	2	16	0	1
$20,000–24,999	4	8	1	18	0	1
$25,000–49,999	4	12	1	20	0	1
$50,000 or more	3	1	2	21	0	0

Source: Authors' calculations from the May 1978 *CPS*.

7· COMPENSATING WAGE DIFFERENTIALS FOR MANDATORY OVERTIME?

The overtime pay premium provisions of the FLSA currently regulate only two dimensions of the hours of work relationship, the number of hours after which the overtime premium goes into effect (forty) and the premium's level (time and a half). In their legislation, several European countries regulate other dimensions; for example, they require either prior governmental approval for overtime, for employees to give their consent to working overtime, or both (National Board for Prices and Incomes 1970).[1] The bill to amend the FLSA introduced into Congress in 1979 by Representative Conyers would similarly have prohibited mandatory assignment of overtime in the United States.

As discussed in Chapter 1, a rationale for many forms of protective labor legislation is that they are attempts to correct for failures of private markets, and overtime hours legislation can be analyzed with this in mind. For even if both employers and their employees were satisfied with long workweeks and no premium pay for overtime, their private calculations ignore the social costs of unemployment. An overtime premium can be thought of as a tax to make employers bear the full marginal social cost of their hours decisions; its intent is to reduce the use of overtime hours and stimu-

---

1. Employee consent for overtime is required in both Belgium and the Netherlands.

late employment growth. The payment of the premium directly to employed workers may be justified if market imperfections prevent workers from freely choosing their desired workweeks and force them to work excessively long hours. The payment can then be seen as an attempt to reduce their disutility from long workweeks.

Proposals to legislate prohibitions against mandatory overtime can be viewed as being based upon the belief that market imperfections persist in the labor market and that the overtime premium does not fully compensate employees for the disutility associated with mandatory overtime. It is questionable, however, if markets have failed here. There appear to be a variety of overtime hours provisions offered in the labor market; for example, as noted in Chapter 3 only 16 percent of the individuals in the *1977 Michigan Quality of Employment Survey (QES)* who reported working overtime also reported that the overtime hours decision was made unilaterally by their employer and that overtime was mandatory in the sense that employees who refused it suffered a penalty. In addition, roughly 20 percent of employees covered by major collective bargaining agreements in 1976 had explicit provisions in their contracts that gave them the right to refuse overtime (table 7.1).[2]

To the extent that labor markets are competitive and establishments do offer a variety of overtime hours provisions (e.g., employer determines, employee determines, penalty for refusal), compensating wage differentials should arise. To attract labor, establishments that offered distasteful mandatory overtime provisions would have to pay higher straight-time wages, higher overtime premiums, or higher fringe benefits than establishments in which such provisions did not occur. If fully compensating wage differentials exist, there is no case for legislative prohibitions against mandatory overtime. Evidence on the extent to which such compensating wage differentials currently do exist is of importance to policy makers.

In this chapter, the *QES* data are used to estimate the extent to which employees currently are compensated, in the form of higher straight-time wages, for being required to work manda-

---

2. Over 50 percent of the workers covered by this provision, however, were in the transportation equipment industry.

tory overtime.[3] The estimating equations are derived from a model in which wage rates and the existence of mandatory assignment of overtime are jointly determined in the market; an employee's supply of mandatory overtime is positively related to the premium he or she would receive for working mandatory overtime, while an employer's demand for mandatory overtime provisions is negatively related to the premium he or she would have to pay to institute this work rule. Such a model leads naturally to the estimation of wage equations, using econometric techniques that correct for the sample selectivity problem (see, for example, Heckman 1979); that is, in the empirical research, an attempt is made to control for the fact that employees and employers are not randomly assigned to the mandatory overtime sector but rather make explicit choices to locate there. An explanation of the statistical problem and the details of both the theoretical model and empirical estimates are found in Appendixes E and F. The findings are summarized here.

Are There Compensating Wage Differentials for Mandatory Overtime?

The goal is to estimate the extent to which individuals employed by firms that require mandatory overtime receive higher straight-time wages than otherwise identical individuals employed by firms in which overtime is voluntary. If the wage of the ith individual is W_{im} if he or she works in a firm in which overtime is mandatory and W_{iv} if he or she works in a firm in which overtime is voluntary, then the relative wage differential received for mandatory overtime d_i can be defined as

$$d_i = (W_{im} - W_{iv})/W_{iv} \approx \log(W_{im}/W_{iv}). \tag{7.1}$$

---

3. These data contain no information on the value of fringes; hence, it is not possible to test if compensating fringe benefit differentials arise. The survey does contain data on the overtime pay premium. Preliminary analyses suggested that the premium was not correlated with the presence of mandatory overtime rules, other variables held constant, when the sample was restricted to individuals who reported they received a premium of at least time and a half. For these reasons, this chapter focuses only on the question of compensating straight-time wage differentials.

In general, it is not possible to observe both W_{im} and W_{iv} with cross section data, as at a point in time an individual is typically employed either by a firm that requires mandatory overtime or by a firm that does not, but not by both. A naïve approach that circumvents this problem is to estimate wage equations separately for individuals in the mandatory and nonmandatory sectors, use the estimated coefficients from these regressions and the characteristics of a representative individual to compute predicted values of the wage rate that the individual would receive in both sectors, and then estimate the differential by calculating the percentage difference in these predicted values.

More formally, suppose that the wage rate an individual would receive in a job requiring mandatory overtime is a log linear function of a vector of variables **X** that represent personal characteristics (e.g., education, experience) and the characteristics of the employer (e.g., union status, establishment size, industry) plus an error term (ϵ_{im})

$$\log W_{im} = \sum_{j=1}^{K} \alpha_{jm} X_{ji} + \varepsilon_{im} \tag{7.2}$$

and that a similar functional relationship describes the wage that an individual would receive in a job in which overtime was voluntary

$$\log W_{iv} = \sum_{j=1}^{K} \alpha_{jv} X_{ji} + \varepsilon_{iv} . \tag{7.3}$$

The naïve approach would involve estimating the parameters of equation 7.2 by ordinary least squares (OLS) from observations of individuals who work mandatory overtime and the parameters of equation 7.3 by OLS from observations of individuals who are not required to work mandatory overtime. Given estimates of these parameters, $\hat{\alpha}_{jm}$, $\hat{\alpha}_{jv}$, and the characteristics of a representative individual and his employer, X_{ji}, an estimate of the relative straight-time wage premium paid for mandatory overtime can then be obtained from

$$\hat{d}_i = \log \hat{W}_{im} - \log \hat{W}_{iv} = \sum_{j=1}^{K} (\hat{\alpha}_{jm} - \hat{\alpha}_{jv}) X_{ji} . \tag{7.4}$$

As is now well known, however, estimates of wage equations from truncated samples will not necessarily yield unbiased estimates of the underlying structural wage equations, since the assumption that the error term in each equation is random and uncorrelated with the other explanatory variables is typically violated (see Heckman 1979 for a more detailed discussion of this point). This occurs because employees and employers are not randomly assigned to the mandatory overtime sector but rather make explicit choices. Estimates of the wage equation that ignore the underlying choice model will be biased because they will confound the effect of an explanatory variable on wages with its effect on the probability that an individual is or is not employed by a firm that requires mandatory overtime. To adequately correct for this sample selectivity problem requires a model of the underlying economic choice process that determines whether an individual is observed working mandatory overtime. This problem is complicated by the fact that such an event is a product of both employee and employer decisions.

A formal model of the economic choice process that determines whether an individual is observed working mandatory overtime, along with a description of the econometric procedure used to correct for the sample selectivity problem, is found in Appendix E.[4] For the interested reader, Appendix F also presents ordinary least square and selectivity corrected estimates of the wage equations that result. Here these analyses are summarized, and the implied percentage straight-time wage premiums paid to workers who are required to work mandatory overtime are presented.

The data used to estimate whether workers who are required to work mandatory overtime are paid higher straight-time wages than otherwise comparable workers who are not required to work mandatory overtime came from the QES. Those individuals who failed to report their straight-time hourly wage rate, whether they were required to work mandatory overtime, or both were eliminated from the original 1,515 individuals in the survey who were employed full-time. An individual was said to be required to work mandatory overtime if he or she reported that he or she could not refuse

---

4. The formal econometric model that is used is based heavily on Poirer 1980. A similar model is found in Abowd and Farber 1978.

to work overtime without a penalty. This left a usable sample of 1,108 observations, of which 165, or 14.89 percent were categorized as being employed in a job that required mandatory overtime.

The wage equations 7.2 and 7.3 were estimated separately for individuals in the mandatory overtime and nonmandatory or voluntary overtime sectors. These equations represent a standard human capital model, augmented by a dichotomous variable indicating on the one hand if the individual is either a union member or not a member but covered by a union contract, and on the other hand if the individual is neither a member nor covered by a contract. Included are measures of the individual's total labor market experience, experience with the current employer, years of formal schooling and trade school, health status, sex, race, and marital status.[5]

The coefficient estimates obtained for these wage equations can be used to compute estimates of the straight-time wage premium paid to workers who are required to work mandatory overtime using equation 7.4. This is done initially for a representative worker who has the *mean* value of each of the characteristics X in the sample. These estimated premiums are tabulated in the top row on table 7.2. The number in the first column is obtained from the unadjusted OLS wage equations; the number in the second column is obtained from the estimated wage equations that correct for selectivity bias.

Quite strikingly, in neither case is the estimated premium positive. While the OLS estimate is close to zero, the selectivity adjusted estimate actually suggests that workers in the mandatory overtime sector may well receive lower straight-time wages. On average, market forces do not seem to be producing a compensating wage differential for mandatory overtime. The fact that on average such a differential does not exist, however, does not imply that *no* workers in the economy are compensated for being required to work mandatory overtime. In particular, one might want to examine whether such differentials exist for employees covered by collective bargaining agreements.

---

5. To ascertain if the estimated differentials were sensitive to the specification of the wage equation used, additional wage equations that included vectors of one-digit occupation and industry dichotomous variables were also estimated. The pattern of differentials that emerged from these equations was quite similar to those reported in the text.

Recently attention has been redirected by Richard Freeman, James Medoff, and their associates to the many roles unions play in addition to simply seeking to increase their members' wages (for an excellent expository survey of their views, see Freeman and Medoff 1979). Empirical studies have indicated that unions may affect productivity and labor turnover (for example, Brown and Medoff 1978, Clark 1980, and Medoff 1979). In addition, it has been argued that unions may help to compensate for market failures by providing information on unfavorable working conditions or obtaining compensating wage differentials for employees who work under such conditions. Indeed, a recent study suggests that up to two-fifths of the estimated union-nonunion wage differential is simply a compensating differential because unionized employees tend to be employed in more structured and hence less desirable (from the perspective of the employees) work settings (Duncan and Stafford 1979).

Following this logic, one might hypothesize that unions will also achieve *larger* compensating wage differentials for their members than those received by otherwise comparable nonunion employees. That is, markets may be sufficiently imperfect that compensating differentials might not arise in the absence of union pressure; unions may help restore the differentials that would exist in the absence of these imperfections.

To test for this possibility with respect to mandatory overtime provisions, the second and third rows of table 7.2 present estimates of the percentage straight-time wage premium paid to workers required to work mandatory overtime in the union and nonunion sectors, respectively. These estimates again make use of the wage equation estimates presented in Appendix F and equation 7.4; the differentials paid to union members are evaluated using the mean values of union members' characteristics, while those for nonunion members are evaluated at the mean values of nonunion employees' characteristics.[6]

As hypothesized, the estimated differentials are positive in the union sector but are negative in the nonunion sector. The OLS

6. Attempts were also made to reestimate the model separately for union and nonunion employees and then to base the estimated differentials on these equations. Unfortunately, the small sample sizes in several of the cells prevented any meaningful results.

estimates suggest that the straight-time wage premium paid to induce workers to accept jobs requiring mandatory overtime is
roughly 4.0 percent in unionized establishments, while the estimates
that control for selectivity bias place the premium at about 2.6 percent. In contrast, regardless of the method of estimation used, nonunion employees who are required to work mandatory overtime fail
to receive a premium for this undesirable working condition.

It is also plausible that whether a premium is paid for mandatory overtime depends upon an employee's job tenure with a firm. If
an employer seeks to attract a new employee to a firm that requires
mandatory overtime, one might hypothesize that a compensating
wage differential will be required. In contrast, employees who have
been with an establishment for a number of years and have accumulated firm-specific human capital may find that there is a wedge between the wage they are receiving and the wage they can command
from other employers in the market (Becker 1964). As such, ex post,
it is not necessarily the case that the employer will have to pay them a
compensating wage differential for the unfavorable working condition if it is newly instituted.[7] Their investments in firm-specific human
capital limit the need for such a differential to arise.

This line of reasoning leads to the hypothesis that compensating wage differentials for mandatory overtime will be larger for
employees with only a few years experience with a firm than they
will be for long-term employees. To test this hypothesis, the sample
was divided into employees with less than three years experience
with their current employer and those with three or more years.
OLS wage equations and the selectivity corrected wage equations
comparable to those found in Appendix F were reestimated for each
group, and then the estimated straight-time wage premium paid to
employers required to work mandatory overtime was computed as
before.

---

7. This statement should be qualified by noting that if ex ante employees
expect to have long tenures with a firm and they are aware that an unfavorable
working condition exists or may be instituted at the firm in the future, then they
would accept employment there only if they expected to receive compensating differentials throughout their tenure with the firm. The argument in the text essentially
assumes that the unfavorable working condition was imposed unexpectedly sometime
after their initial hire dates.

These estimated differentials are evaluated at the mean values of the characteristics for the individuals in each group and are reported in the last two rows of table 7.2. Again, the hypothesis appears to be borne out, at least for the OLS estimates. These estimates suggest that positive compensating differentials for mandatory overtime are paid to inexperienced workers with less than three years of job tenure, while no such differential is paid to workers with more than three years job tenure. In contrast, the estimates corrected for selectivity suggest that neither group receives a positive compensating differential for mandatory overtime.

In sum, the results in this section indicate that on average employees who work for establishments with mandatory overtime provisions do not receive compensatingly higher straight-time wages. Focusing on what happens on average, however, masks important differences between groups. The data suggest that unionized employees do receive a straight-time wage premium for mandatory overtime; this provides support for the view that one role of unions is to establish compensating wage differentials for unfavorable working conditions (Duncan and Stafford 1980). The data also provide some support for the view that experienced workers, who are "tied" to firms, fail to receive compensating wage differentials for mandatory overtime, while workers with less than three years experience with a firm do receive such a differential.

Are Compensating Wage Differentials Fully Compensating?

Are the magnitudes of these differentials for unionized employees and employees with short job tenures sufficient to fully compensate them for mandatory overtime provisions? A long and growing literature in labor economics provides evidence on the existence of compensating wage differentials for various job characteristics. Among the characteristics examined have been risk of injury (Smith 1976 and Thaler and Rosen 1975), nonwage forms of compensation, such as retirement system characteristics (Ehrenberg 1980), working conditions (Duncan 1976 and Duncan and Stafford 1980), and risk of unemployment (Abowd and Ashenfelter 1979). In some cases, it is possible to test whether the compensating differential is indeed fully compensating. For example, Ehrenberg (1980) found that, holding wages, promised retirement benefits, and the determinants of total conpensation constant, for every dollar that public employees were required to contribute to their pension fund, their annual earnings increased by a dollar. The conclusion that the wage differential associated with employee's retirement system contributions is fully compensating is a straightforward one in this case.

In other situations it is not easy to establish whether compensating differentials are fully compensating. Estimates of the compensating differential associated with the risk of fatal injury at the workplace suggest that individuals are paid a premium of 1 to 4 percent of their wages to compensate them for risks of fatal injuries (Smith 1979). But researchers have not evaluated whether such differentials truly fully compensate workers for the risks of fatal injury; they are simply the differentials observed in the market. If labor markets are not perfectly competitive, there is no reason to assume that the differentials are in fact fully compensating.

In the present case, it is possible to evaluate whether the compensating differentials observed for mandatory overtime are fully compensating. Figure 7.1 plots a familiar labor supply model. Suppose an individual has nonlabor income of OT and a wage rate of W for the first $\bar{H}$ hours worked per week, and that he or she received an overtime premium of time and half for all overtime hours worked. The individual then faces the budget constraint $BAOT$ and given his or her indifference map, where utility is assumed to be a function of income and leisure, the individual will locate at point a, work H_0 hours and have a total income of Y_0.[8] Thus, his or her utility is given by

$$U(Y_0, L_0). \tag{7.5}$$

Now suppose the individual was employed by a firm in which mandatory overtime was required and was forced to work $H_1 - H_0$ more hours of overtime than he or she otherwise would choose. It is easy to see that each value of a straight-time wage premium for mandatory overtime d will lead to a new budget line and that there is

8. The assumption that the individual would voluntarily choose to work overtime is not essential to what follows.

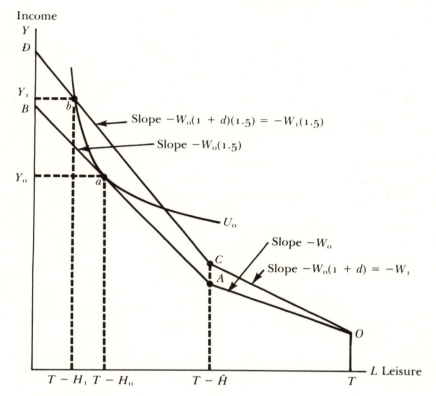

FIGURE 7.1
Fully Compensating Wage Differential
for Mandatory Overtime

only one value of d which will permit him or her to locate at point b where income will be Y_1 and where

$$U(Y_1, L_1) = U(Y_0, L_0). \tag{7.6}$$

This value of d, which leads to the budget line $DCOT$, is the differential that fully compensates the individual for mandatory overtime. Provided that the individual's marginal utilities from income and leisure are both positive and his or her indifference curves are convex, higher values of d will more than fully compensate the employee, while lesser values will less than fully compensate him or her. Furthermore, how onerous mandatory overtime is depends upon the difference between H_1 and H_0; the larger this gap, the larger will be the straight-time wage premium necessary to fully compensate the employee for mandatory overtime.[9]

Of course to implement this approach and to estimate the fully compensating straight-time wage differential is no trivial task. Any given individual either works for a firm requiring mandatory overtime or does not. Hence, one can directly observe *either* W_0 and H_0, or W_1 ($=W_0(1+d)$) and H_1, but not both. Furthermore, it is necessary to know the shape of the individual's indifference curve, something which is typically not directly observed.

There is a method by which all the necessary information can be deduced. This method is detailed in Appendix G; suffice it to say here that it requires the assumption of a specific functional form for the individual's indifference curve and then the estimation of the parameters of that function. Using this method, the data suggest that a fully compensating straight-time wage differential for mandatory overtime is approximately 1.1 percent.

This estimate is somewhat less than the estimates of 2.6 to 4.0 percent for the differentials obtained for unionized workers and also less than the OLS estimated differential of 3.1 percent obtained for inexperienced workers (table 7.2). While it would be interesting to ascertain how sensitive the fully compensating differential is to the functional form of the utility function assumed, these results suggest that on average for these workers the market has worked quite well. On average, compensating wage differentials for mandatory overtime appear to be fully compensating for unionized employees and for workers with short job tenure with their current employers.

Conclusions

Do employees who are employed by firms in which mandatory assignment of overtime is required receive compensating straight-time wage differentials? The evidence presented in this chapter suggests

---

9. This analysis assumes that the individual is concerned about total hours of leisure in a week, not how it is allocated across days. If the employee were concerned about the latter, it is conceivable that he or she would require a premium to be employed by a firm requiring mandatory overtime even if H_0 was equal to H_1. This complication is not dealt with here.

that on average they do not and provides some support for the case in favor of legislative prohibition of mandatory overtime. This conclusion should be qualified, however, because for unionized employees and employees with short job tenure with their current employers, compensating wage differentials do exist. Moreover, the magnitude of these differentials appear to be sufficiently large to be fully compensating. The case for the legislation, then, is strongest for the nonunion sector. Of course, even here the benefits from the legislation must be weighed against the potential costs; these include reduced employer flexibility in scheduling production, increased production costs, and therefore reduced employment.

It would be less than honest not to acknowledge three major qualifications of the findings reported in this chapter. First, it is conceivable that the model used to determine full compensation understates the true magnitude of the fully compensating wage differential. That model assumes that individuals value only income and leisure time; the disutility from mandatory overtime provisions arises because employees are forced to work more hours than they otherwise would prefer. Suppose, however, the employees also value the way in which overtime hours are distributed across a week and mandatory overtime provisions cause them to lose control over this decision (e.g., "you can't work one hour overtime a day like you want but you have to work five hours on Monday night"). In this case, even if total hours of work were unchanged, employees would still demand a premium for accepting mandatory overtime provisions. The model does not capture the need for such a premium.

Second, software limitations have at least temporarily prevented the estimation of the complete statistical model that Appendix E indicates is required to control for the sample selection problem; the consistency properties of the selectivity adjusted wage equations and the associated wage differentials reported in table 7.2 are conditional upon the approximation used (see Appendix E). In addition, the simulations of the fully compensating wage differentials assume a very simple, and restrictive, functional form for the utility function (Appendix G). In future work, tests will be made of the sensitivity of these results to the specification of the utility function used and attempts made to ascertain if estimating the more complete selection model alters any of the present conclusions.

Finally, it should be noted that the desirable statistical properties of the selectivity corrected estimates hinge on correct specification of both the variables that enter the wage and the selection equations and the functional forms of these equations. To the extent that errors have occurred, it is not obvious whether the selectivity corrected estimates or the least squares estimates are to be preferred.

TABLE 7.1
Overtime Provisions in
Major Collective
Bargaining Agreements, 1976

	Number	Workers Covered
Total number of agreements	1,570	6,741,750
Daily overtime provisions	1,393	6,069,750
Time and a half	1,243	5,552,000
Double time	105	350,800
After 8 hours a day	1,268	5,266,650
Weekly overtime provisions	997	4,393,750
Time and a half	942	4,222,300
Double time	33	106,450
After fewer than 40 hours a week	54	209,350
Overtime outside regularly scheduled hours	570	2,153,300
Graduated overtime rates	370	1,518,350
Equal distribution of overtime	661	2,832,700
Right to refuse overtime[a]	280	1,346,650
Premium pay for weekends	1,430	6,070,400
Saturday not part of regular workweek	880	3,741,400
more than time and a half	171	533,400
Sunday not part of regular workweek	1,211	5,136,200
more than time and a half	871	3,461,550
Saturday part of regular workweek	39	104,400
Sunday part of regular workweek	193	1,545,850

Source: U.S., Bureau of Labor Statistics 1979.
Note: [a]Over 50 percent of the workers covered by this provision are in the transportation equipment industry.

TABLE 7.2

Percentage Straight-Time Wage Premium
Paid for Mandatory Overtime, 1977

	Estimates from OLS Equations	Estimates from Equations Corrected for Selectivity Bias
All workers[a]	−0.6%	−3.5%
Union workers[a]	4.0	2.6
Nonunion workers[a]	−3.0	−7.0
Less than 3 years with current employer[b]	3.1	−2.3
3 or more years with current employer[b]	−7.3	−11.5

Source: Authors' calculations based on the 1977 *QES*.
Notes: The sample sizes are shown below.

	All, Union, Nonunion Workers	Less than 3 yrs. with Employer	3 or more yrs. with Employer
Mandatory sector	165	68	97
Nonmandatory sector	943	434	509

Examples of the wage equations that underlie this table are found in appendix table F.1.

[a]Separate wage equations were estimated for those people who worked mandatory overtime and those who did not. The differentials are evaluated in "all workers" using the mean values of the explanatory variables for all workers, in "union workers" using the mean values of union workers' characteristics, and in "nonunion workers' the mean values of nonunion workers' characteristics.

[b]The two wage equations, mandatory and nonmandatory, were estimated separately for new and experienced workers and the differentials computed in an analogous manner.

8· SHOULD THE OVERTIME PAY PROVISIONS OF THE FLSA BE AMENDED?

Previous studies, and this one, have demonstrated that across establishments, a strong positive relationship exists between the use of overtime hours and the ratio of weekly nonwage labor costs per employee to the overtime wage rate. They imply that increasing the overtime premium to double time would substantially reduce the use of overtime hours, perhaps by as much as 20 percent, if compliance with the legislation did not change and if straight-time wage rates were not affected. Moreover, to the extent that the reduction in hours could be converted into new full-time employment, such a change in the legislation has the potential to increase employment of workers subject to the overtime provisions by perhaps 1 or 2 percent.

Whether such an increase in employment would actually occur and whether the new jobs would go to currently nonemployed individuals is another matter. This study presents evidence on a number of factors that might reduce the job creation aspects of the proposal: nonzero wage elasticities of demand for labor, the possibility of increased moonlighting, the similarity or lack of similarity between the skill distributions of the unemployed and those who work overtime, indivisibilities associated with integrated team production processes and with establishment size, the possibility of increased noncompliance with the legislation, and the possibility that compensating variations in straight-time wages might occur. It also examines the income distribution consequences of such a proposal. In summarizing the evidence and drawing conclusions about the wisdom of raising the overtime premium to double time, requiring the premium to be paid after thirty-five hours, or prohibiting mandatory overtime, the reader should bear in mind two general observations.

First, an overtime pay premium may be thought of as a tax to make employers bear the full marginal social cost of their hours decisions; in the premium's absence employers' calculations ignore the costs borne by society due to unemployment. It does not necessarily follow, however, that the revenue that would accrue from any increase in the tax should be distributed to employees in the form of higher premium pay for overtime. Indeed, over the years several proposals have suggested that the revenue from any increase in the tax on overtime go directly to the unemployed, in the sense that it be contributed either to the unemployment insurance fund, to employment and training program budgets, or to both (see U.S., Department of Labor 1967 and Young 1978).[1] Such proposals make a good deal of sense. Unless it can be demonstrated that market imperfections prevent currently employed workers from freely choosing the length of their workweeks and that the existing overtime premium does not fully compensate these workers for the disutility associated with long workweeks, then no increase in the premium paid to employees is justified. One can thus logically be in favor of raising the tax paid by employers when they use overtime hours but not in favor of raising the overtime premium paid to employees.

Second, even if one ultimately can show that increasing the overtime premium would lead to a substantial increase in employment of individuals who were initially not employed, it does not necessarily follow that the policy should be implemented. Presumably other policies, such as the use of marginal employee tax credits, could accomplish the same goal (Eisner 1978). The distribution of costs associated with the two types of legislation, however, would be different. In the former case, the costs would be borne by consumers

---

1. Howard Young, who was a special consultant to the president of the United Auto Workers, favored both raising the overtime premium to double time and instituting an additional surtax on overtime paid by the employer directly into a social welfare fund. Most recently this position was supported by Kenneth Morris, a regional director of the United Auto Workers, in his testimony on the Conyers bill (U.S., House of Representatives 1980).

of products produced in industries where overtime was worked (higher prices), owners of these industries (lower profits), and employees (less overtime but at higher pay). In the latter case, the costs would be borne primarily by taxpayers and consumers at large in the form of higher taxes to fund the deficit induced by the tax credit, or in the form of higher rates of inflation, or both. What are required are benefit-cost analyses of alternative policies designed to accomplish a given objective (such as these two), not merely evidence that a single policy option will have a postulated impact.

Should the Overtime Premium Be Raised to Double Time?

The evidence presented in Chapters 2 through 6 probably does not support proposals to increase the overtime premium to double time as a means of stimulating employment. The econometric analyses of the BLS *1976 Employer Expenditure for Employee Compensation* data and the simulations that followed from these analyses suggested that the *maximum* employment gain that would result from the increase in the premium would be in the range of 0.5 to 1.5 percent in manufacturing and 0.8 to 2.1 percent in nonmanufacturing.[2]

It must be remembered, however, that the employment base here is not *all* payroll employees, but rather employees subject to the overtime pay provisions of the legislation; and as table 1.1 indicates, only 58 percent of all employees were covered by the legislation in 1977. Moreover, the attempts to directly estimate the effect of a change in the overtime wage rate on overtime hours in manufacturing—to separate the independent effects of the overtime premium from the effects of the weekly quasi-fixed costs of labor on overtime hours—met with failure. The simulated employment effects reported for manufacturing may be only an artifact of constraining the

---

2. Significantly larger estimated effects were obtained by estimating models in which the usage of overtime hours and the ratio of quasi-fixed weekly labor costs to the overtime wage rate were assumed to be simultaneously determined. However, these employment effects were derived from 2SLS estimates that suggested, at least for manufacturing, that an increase in overtime hours leads firms to *lower* the quasi-fixed costs/overtime wage rate ratio. This latter result is contrary to a priori expectations (see Chapter 2); this suggests that the research failed to adequately identify both the overtime hours and the quasi-fixed costs/overtime wage rate equations. Therefore, much more confidence should be placed in the results reported above.

effects of a 1 percent increase in the quasi-fixed costs and in the overtime wage on overtime hours to be equal and opposite in sign, a constraint that was rejected by formal statistical tests. While this problem did not arise in the nonmanufacturing data, this should lower confidence that increasing the overtime premium would reduce overtime and increase employment in the manufacturing sector.

Furthermore, it must be remembered that these estimated employment gains are maximum estimates of the number of jobs that would be created and go to nonemployed workers. These estimates were predicated on six assumptions; if any of these fail to hold, the estimated employment gains would be reduced. Chapters 3 through 5 analyzed the evidence on the validity of these assumptions and concluded that while some of the assumptions are valid, on balance, the failure of them would substantially reduce the actual employment gain associated with an increase in the overtime premium. Each of these assumptions is discussed in turn.

First, the maximum employment gain estimates assume that employers' wage elasticities of demand for labor are completely inelastic and thus that any reduction in overtime hours would be converted to new jobs. An increase in the overtime premium, however, does raise the average cost per man-hour of labor; this should lead to a shift to more capital intensive means of production and, to the extent that the cost increase is passed on to consumers in the form of higher prices, to a reduction in output. Both effects should lead to a decline in the number of man-hours demanded by employers, and the simulations based on previous estimates of the wage elasticity of demand for labor suggest that this factor should cause the estimate of the number of new jobs created to fall by 0.25 percentage points.

Second, the estimated employment effects assume that all the new jobs that would be created would go to individuals who were unemployed. This ignores the possibility of increased moonlighting by currently employed workers who are working overtime in response to a simultaneous increase in the overtime premium and a decrease in their overtime hours. If this occurred, the actual employment gains would be reduced. Simulations based on previous studies of moonlighting decisions suggest, however, that increased moonlighting would not significantly restrict the number of any newly created jobs that would go to the unemployed.

Third, the employment gain estimates assume that indivisibilities in production processes will not prevent any reduction in overtime hours from being converted to new full-time jobs. For example, while large establishments may have the option of substituting one new full-time employee for the overtime hours of twenty employees who each work two overtime hours a week, small establishments with only a few employees working overtime may not enjoy such options. If such constraints existed, one might contemplate exempting small establishments from any increase in the overtime premium; this would reduce the estimated employment gain associated with an increase in the premium. The only previous study that looked at the issue, however, found no systematic relationship between establishment size and the existence of a trade-off between overtime hours and employment (Ehrenberg 1971a).

Fourth, the employment gain simulations reported in Chapter 2 assume that an increase in the overtime premium will not lead to compensating adjustments in straight-time wages or fringe benefits. Suppose, however, that firms and their employees were initially in an equilibrium situation in which overtime hours were regularly scheduled. One plausible response to a legislated increase in the premium is for them to voluntarily agree to a reduction in the level of straight-time wages, or fringes, or both, leaving total compensation for the initial number of hours unchanged. If this occurred, it may be argued that neither side would have an incentive to reduce the usage of overtime (the legislation would have had no effect on the employer's total cost or on the employee's total compensation for the given number of hours) and the resulting employment gain would be reduced. While this study was unable to obtain any evidence on the probability that such compensating wage or fringe benefit differentials would arise, at least one previous study has found that increases in the minimum wage sometimes lead to compensating reductions in fringe benefits. Thus, this possibility should not be dismissed out of hand.

Fifth, these estimates assume that the skill distributions of those working overtime and those who are unemployed are sufficiently similar that bottlenecks will not arise. Put another way, they assume that there will always be unemployed workers available to fill the newly created positions. But comparisons that were made in Chapter 4 of the distributions of the experienced unemployed by skill class and geographic area and the similar distribution for those working overtime, using data from the May 1978 *Current Population Survey (CPS)*, suggest that bottlenecks may well arise. Indeed, the data suggest that at least 8.5 percent of all the newly created jobs would go unfilled for want of workers with the required skills residing in the same geographic area. This estimate is subject to a number of qualifications, however, and the importance of the skill bottleneck problem will depend on the stage of the business cycle that the economy is in. In periods of higher unemployment when less overtime is worked, skill mismatches would be less a problem, and vice versa.

Finally, the maximum employment gain estimates assume both that the overtime pay provisions of the FLSA are fully complied with and that an increase in the overtime premium would not reduce the compliance rate. In fact, analyses of the May 1978 *CPS* data and the *1977 Michigan Quality of Employment Survey (QES)* data suggest that at least 10 to 20 percent of the employees working overtime who should legally receive a premium of time and a half for overtime fail to receive it. If the noncompliance rate were to remain constant in response to an increase in the premium to double time and employers continued to pay these employees the same premium, employers' usage of overtime hours would not change, and the estimated employment gain estimates would be reduced by 10 to 20 percent.

Taken together, these factors suggest that the employment gain associated with an increase in the overtime premium is likely to be considerably less than the maximum estimates reported in Chapter 2. Furthermore, the analyses of the income distributional consequences of the legislation in Chapter 4 suggest that middle-income and upper income families would gain more from an increase in the overtime premium than would lower income families. More specifically, the analyses of the May 1978 *CPS* data suggest that overtime earnings per family increase with family income and that the net effect of an increase in the overtime premium (taking account of the increased premium rate, the decreased overtime hours, and the increased employment) would be to increase average family income more for middle-income and upper income families than it would for lower income families. When the inflationary consequences of the legislation are added in, the case for increasing the overtime premium to double time is substantially weakened.[3]

Should the Standard Workweek Be Reduced to Thirty-Five Hours?

Should employers be required to pay an overtime pay premium of time and a half after thirty-five hours a week, instead of after forty hours per week as the FLSA currently calls for?[4] The BLS *Employer Expenditure for Employee Compensation* data contained no information on the number of hours a week after which the overtime premium went into effect for each establishment. Hence, it was not possible to estimate the effects of changing this variable on weekly hours per employee and the employment level, as was possible for a change in the overtime premium. As a result, firm conclusions about the desirability of this proposal can not be offered.

It should be emphasized, however, that all the qualifications noted about the earlier simulations would also apply here. For example, the requirement that employers pay time and a half after the first thirty-five hours per week would increase the average hourly wage cost of the first forty hours per employee by 6.25 percent. If the requirement were for double time, the average hourly wage for the first forty hours would increase by 12.5 percent. In either case, employers' would reduce the total man-hours they demand, and this would limit the positive employment effects of the legislated change.

Similarly, converting the hours between thirty-six to forty into overtime hours would increase employers' incentives not to comply with the legislation and lead to possible compensating decreases in straight-time wages and fringes. Both these changes would reduce employer's incentives to substitute increased employment for overtime hours. Finally, one would again have to consider the possibility

---

3. In Chapter 3, it was calculated that such an increase in the premium might increase average hourly labor wage costs by 0.8 percent for workers covered by the legislation. Whether this would have a large enough impact on prices to worry about is open to question. In the authors' view, it would.

4. As table 7.1 indicates, only 3.1 percent of all employees covered by major collective bargaining agreements in 1976 had contracts which called for the premium to go into effect before forty hours per week.

that skill mismatches between the unemployed and the new jobs that were created would constrain the employment effects of the change in the legislation. Of course, since this amendment would apply to all covered full-time workers, not solely those working more than forty hours, it is less likely that skill mismatches would be a problem in this case. Put another way, the skill mix of the experienced unemployed is much more similar to the skill mix of all covered full-time workers than it is to the skill mix of those working overtime.

Should Mandatory Overtime Be Prohibited?

Should mandatory assignment of overtime be prohibited? Should employers be required to obtain the consent of their employees or their employees' representative before they can assign employees to work overtime? Proponents of such an amendment argue that it would restore freedom of choice over work hours to employees, a freedom that is lacking in many situations. Opponents argue that such an amendment would reduce employers' flexibility in scheduling production, increase their costs of production, and reduce the international competitiveness of American industry.

It is doubtful whether such a provision would be enforceable. Employers could presumably still require willingness to work mandatory overtime as a condition of employment, and if this was agreed to at the date of hire, it is hard to see what the net effect of the legislation would be. This consideration aside, the case for prohibitions against mandatory overtime is based upon the belief that market imperfections persist in labor markets and that the overtime premium does not fully compensate employees for the disutility associated with mandatory overtime.

It is not obvious that markets have failed in this area; there appear to be a variety of overtime hours provisions offered in the labor market. However, the analyses of the *QES* data in Chapter 7 do lend some support to the market failure argument. They suggest that, on average, establishments that offer distasteful mandatory overtime provisions do not have to pay higher straight-time wages to attract labor than do establishments in which such provisions do not exist. The absence of such compensating wage differentials clearly strengthens the case for legislated prohibitions against mandatory overtime.

This conclusion should be qualified, however, because the estimates suggest that compensating wage differentials do exist for unionized workers and for newly hired workers; in these cases, the magnitude of the differentials appears to be sufficiently large to "fully" compensate unionized and new employees for the disutility of mandatory overtime provisions. Since the labor market appears to work well for new hires and unionized employees, the case in favor of such an amendment is strongest for nonunion employees, especially experienced ones. For the reasons discussed earlier, however, whether the FLSA should be amended in such a manner for this more limited group is not obvious.

APPENDIXES

A · 2SLS ESTIMATES OF OVERTIME AND FRINGE/OVERTIME EQUATIONS

TABLE A.1

2SLS Estimates of Annual Overtime and Fringe/Overtime Wage Equations: 1976 *EEC* Data
(absolute value *t* statistics in parentheses)

Explanatory Variables	Manufacturing			Nonmanufacturing[a]		
	$\log(OT)$	$\log(OT)$	$\log(F_1/W_1)$	$\log(OT)$	$\log(OT)$	$\log(F_1/W_1)$
$\log(OT)$			−0.397 (2.3)			0.398 (5.4)
$\log(F_1/W_1)$	1.760 (5.5)	2.116 (5.2)		1.633(5.6)	1.772(5.9)	
Z6	−2.049 (0.5)	−3.766 (0.9)		−22.829(5.4)	−19.944(4.5)	
Z7	−0.102 (0.7)	−0.062 (0.4)		−0.469(3.1)	−0.418(2.8)	
Z23	1.123 (3.7)	1.375 (4.2)	0.042 (0.8)	0.039(0.2)	.100(0.4)	0.127 (2.6)
Z24	−0.256 (2.6)	−0.347 (3.3)	0.271 (2.8)	−0.077(0.5)	−.103(0.7)	0.204 (2.9)
R9			0.043 (0.2)			
E1		0.032 (0.1)	−0.323 (2.6)		0.374(1.6)	−0.212 (2.0)
E2		−0.414 (2.4)	−0.112 (1.6)		0.245(1.8)	−0.087 (1.4)
E3		−0.097 (0.7)	0.010 (0.1)		0.239(1.6)	−0.094 (1.4)
E5		0.216 (1.5)	0.167 (2.1)		−0.120(0.6)	0.116 (1.4)
E6		0.123 (0.8)	0.091 (1.2)		0.074(0.4)	0.078 (1.0)
E7		−0.227 (1.4)	0.026 (0.2)		−0.049(0.3)	0.133 (1.8)
E8		−0.048 (0.2)	0.270 (1.8)		0.059(0.3)	0.170 (1.8)
E9		−0.341 (1.0)			0.246(0.9)	0.051 (0.4)

TABLE A.1 (*continued*)

Explanatory Variables	Manufacturing			Nonmanufacturing[a]		
	$\log (OT)$	$\log (OT)$	$\log (F_1/W_1)$	$\log (OT)$	$\log (OT)$	$\log (F_1/W_1)$
A1			−0.401 (0.3)			0.046 (0.8)
A2			−1.703 (0.8)			−0.017 (0.5)
A4			−0.666 (2.9)			0.006 (1.1)
A5			−0.063 (0.1)			−0.032 (1.7)
A6			−3.295 (1.5)			−0.228 (1.4)
A10 (× 1,000)			0.049 (1.9)			0.022 (0.4)
F/R^2	7.52/.058	4.12/0.82	6.41/.155	28.85/.181	11.66/.191	16.77/.308
n	614	614	614	658	658	658

Notes: *OT* Annual overtime hours per man.

F_1/W_1. Ratio of weekly quasi-fixed costs per man to the overtime wage rate.

Z6 Sick leave hours as a fraction of sick leave plus working hours.

Z7 1 = standard workweek is 40 hours or less; 0 = otherwise.

Z23 Fraction of employees with less than one week vacation.

Z24 1 = unionized establishment; 0 = otherwise.

R9 Logarithm of average hourly wage in the establishment.

E1 1 if establishment size is <20 employees; 0 = otherwise.

E2 1 if establishment size is 20 to 49 employees; 0 = otherwise.

E3 1 if establishment size is 50 to 99 employees; 0 = otherwise.

E5 1 if establishment size is 250 to 499 employees; 0 = otherwise.

E6 1 if establishment size is 500 to 999 employees; 0 = otherwise.

E7 1 if establishment size is 1,000 to 2,499 employees; 0 = otherwise.

E9) 1 if establishment size is 2,500 or more employees; 0 = otherwise.

A1 Fraction of employees in the industry age 45 or older.

A2 Fraction of employees in the industry age 30 or younger.

A4 Fraction of employees in the industry who are female.

A5 Fraction of employees in the industry who are black.

A6 Fraction of employees in the industry who are Spanish speaking.

A10 Median family income of employees in the industry.

[a]Establishments with positive overtime only.

B · SIMULATING EFFECT ON MOONLIGHTING OF PREMIUM INCREASE AND REDUCTION IN OVERTIME HOURS

Robert Shishko and Bernard Rostker (1976) specify a model of the form

$$h_m = a_0 + a_1 W_m + a_2 W_p + a_3 h_p + a_4 I + \mathbf{a_5' X} + \epsilon \qquad \text{(B.1)}$$

where

h_m = weekly hours on second job
W_m = hourly wage rate on the second job
W_p = hourly wage rate on the primary job
h_p = weekly hours on the primary job
I = $\begin{array}{l}(W_m - W_p)h_p \text{ for specification A} \\ W_p h_p + Z \text{ for specification B}\end{array}$
Z = labor income earned by members of the family other than the head of the household
$\mathbf{X}$ = a vector of descriptive variables including age and family size
ϵ = an error term.

Since the distribution of moonlighting hours is truncated at 0 hours, Shishko and Rostker utilize Tobit analyses. If, for expositional convenience, all the explanatory variables are placed in a vector $\mathbf{X}$, the model may be written:

$$h_m = \mathbf{a'} \, \mathbf{X} + \epsilon$$

Now in the Tobit model, a change in any of the predetermined variables, say X_k, is given by

$$\frac{\partial h_m}{\partial X_k} = a_k \Phi\left(\frac{\mathbf{a'X}}{\sigma}\right) \qquad \text{(B.2)}$$

where a_k is the coefficient of X_k and $\Phi(\cdot)$ is the cumulative normal density function. More precisely,

$$\frac{\partial E(h_m | \mathbf{X})}{\partial X_k} = a_k \Phi\left(\frac{\mathbf{a}'\mathbf{X}}{\sigma}\right).$$

This is *not* conditional on h_m. It represents both the change in moonlighting hours for individuals who were already moonlighting and the change in the number of individuals moonlighting.

Similarly, the elasticity is given by

$$\frac{\partial h_m}{\partial X_k} \cdot \frac{X_k}{h_m} = \frac{a_k X_k \Phi(\mathbf{a}'\mathbf{X}/\sigma)}{h_m} \tag{B.3}$$

Shishko and Rostker report in their table 3 elasticity estimates for all of their variables. The important elasticities for present purposes are given in the following table.

Predetermined Variable	$\dfrac{\partial h_m}{\partial X_k} \cdot \dfrac{X_k}{h_m}$	
	Specification A	Specification B
W_p	−.126	−.862
h_p	−1.406	−1.255
I	.074	−.175

Clearly, the percentage change in moonlighting hours for any specified percentage change in each of these predetermined variables can be approximated by

$$\%\Delta h_m = \frac{\Delta h_m}{h_m} = \left(\frac{\partial h_m}{\partial W_p} \cdot \frac{W_p}{h_m}\right) \cdot \frac{\Delta W_p}{W_p} + \left(\frac{\partial h_m}{\partial h_p} \cdot \frac{h_p}{h_m}\right) \cdot \frac{\Delta h_p}{h_p}$$

$$+ \left(\frac{\partial h_m}{\partial I} \cdot \frac{I}{h_m}\right) \cdot \frac{\Delta I}{I}. \tag{B.4}$$

Since the terms in parentheses are the elasticities tabulated above, all that remains to be indicated is the percentage changes in W_p, h_p, and I induced by a change in the overtime premium.

Suppose that weekly hours on an individual's primary job fall from forty-four per week to forty-two when the overtime premium increases from time and one half to double time. Define the mean wage on the primary job ask

$$\overline{W}_p = ((\text{regular hours})(\text{regular wage})$$
$$+ (\text{overtime hours})(\text{overtime premium})(\text{regular wage}))$$
$$/((\text{regular hours}) + (\text{overtime hours})) \qquad \text{(B.5)}$$

If the overtime premium goes into effect after forty hours per week, then since the mean value of the straight-time primary wage in Shishko and Rostker's sample is \$3.77, the equation yields

$$\overline{W}_p^0 = \frac{(40)(3.77) + (4)(1.5)(3.77)}{44} = \frac{173.42}{44} = \$3.9414$$

$$\overline{W}_p^1 = \frac{(40)(3.77) + (2)(2)(3.77)}{42} = \frac{165.88}{42} = \$3.9495$$

Next, consider the interaction terms. Under specification A, making use of the fact that the mean value of the moonlighting wage is \$3.40, these are

$$I_A^0 = (W_m^0 - W_p^0)h_p^0$$
$$= (3.40 - 3.9495)(44) = -23.82$$
$$I_A^1 = (3.40 - 3.9495)(42) = -23.08 . \qquad \text{(B.6)}$$

Under the assumption that labor income earned by others in the household does not change, the analogous values of the interaction term under specification B are

$$I_B^0 = W_p h_p + Z$$
$$= (3.9414)(44) = 173.42 + Z$$
$$I_B^1 = (3.9495)(42) = 165.88 + Z . \qquad \text{(B.7)}$$

Thus, the relevant percent changes to be used are:

$$\frac{\Delta h_p}{h_p} = \frac{42 - 44}{44} = -4.45\%$$

$$\frac{\Delta W_p}{W_p} = \frac{3.9495 - 3.9414}{3.9414} = 0.207\%$$

$$\frac{\Delta I_A}{I_A} = \frac{(-23.08) - (-23.82)}{-23.82} = -3.107\%$$

$$\frac{\Delta I_B}{I_B} = \frac{165.88 - 173.42}{173.42} = -4.348\%.[1]$$

(B.8)

Substituting the results from equations B.8 and the parameters from the table into equation B.4, the percentage change in moonlighting hours under specification A is given by

$$\%\Delta h_m = (-.126)(.207) + (-1.406)(-4.454) + (.074)$$
$$(-3.107) = 6.13\%$$

(B.9)

and that under specification B,

$$\%\Delta h_m = (-.862)(.207) + (-1.255)(-4.545) +$$
$$(-.175)(-3.107) = 6.07\%$$

(B.10)

Taken together, they suggest that the best estimate is that the simultaneous increase in the overtime premium and the reduction in overtime hours would increase moonlighting hours by approximately 6 percent.

---

1. Note that this is an approximation since the exact term for $\Delta I_B/I_B$ is given by:

$$\frac{\Delta I_B}{I_B} = \frac{(165.88 + Z) - (173.42 + Z)}{173.42 + Z} = \frac{165.88 - 173.42}{173.42 + Z}$$

Unfortunately, the mean value of Z in the sample was not reported. The approximation used above assumed that $Z = 0$. Thus, $\Delta I_B/I_B = -4.348\%$ represents an upper bound. To obtain a lower bound, let Z approach ∞. This implies that $\Delta I_B/I_B$ is close to 0, and that a lower bound for the percentage change in moonlighting hours under specification B is

$$\%\Delta h_m = (-.862)(.207) + (-1.255)(-4.545) = 5.53\%.$$

C · DETERMINING COVERAGE UNDER THE OVERTIME PROVISIONS OF THE FLSA

At its outset, this study required indentification of which individuals in the May 1978 *Current Population Survey* (*CPS*) and the 1977 *Michigan Quality of Employment Survey* (*QES*) data were both covered by the overtime provisions of the FLSA and not exempt from them. Individuals were divided into three categories: Those who were covered with certainty, those for whom coverage could only be guessed at with some probability, and those who either were not covered by or were exempt from the legislation (including the self-employed) or about whom no statement could be made. Analyses were conducted in the text separately for individuals in the first two categories; individuals in the third category were not included in the sample.

The list of exemptions comes from table 13 of the 1978 *Minimum Wage and Maximum Hours Standards under the Fair Labor Standards Act* report, which also provided discussion of how the 1977 amendments to the FLSA changed the exemptions (pp. 7–8). The House of Representatives document *Fair Labor Standards Act of 1938 (As Amended by the Fair Labor Standards Amendments of 1974)* was consulted for a more detailed description of the exemptions as of January 1, 1978. The notes that follow indicate how the various exemptions were accounted for.

1. *Section 13a(1)—Employees in bona fide executive, administrative or professional capacities*
   Exclude individuals with occupation codes 001 to 245 from the sample.[1]

2. *Section 13a(1)—Outside Salespersons*
   Unfortunately it is not possible to separate outside salespersons from other salesworkers. Therefore, it was necessary to exclude all salespersons from the analysis. Exclude

---

1. All the occupation and industry codes used in this appendix refer to those found in the Census of Population.

individuals with occupation codes 260 to 296 from the sample.

3. *State and Local Government Employees except Public Transit, Other Public Utilities, Water Transport Services and State Liquor Stores*
Exclude individuals with industry codes 927, 937 from the sample.

4. *Section 6f and 7l—Domestic Service Workers with Earnings Too Low to be Covered by Social Security*
Exclude from the sample if industry code 769 and earnings are too low to be covered by social security. Since the earnings cutoff was $260 a year, in practice all domestic service workers working overtime were included.

5. *Section 13a(2)—Retail and Service Establishments*
These procedures rely heavily on a June 15, 1978, memorandum from Jack Karlin of the Employment Services Administration to Al Bauman of the Bureau of Labor Statistics. It listed those nonfarm establishments in retail trade and the service sector covered by the overtime provisions by SIC code (transferred into census industry codes below) and size class. In the service sector, some industries were covered for all size classes (727–48, 779, 838, 848–77, 887–97); these were included in the "covered with certainty" sample. In retail trade, one industry was completely excluded from coverage (639, motor vehicle dealers). For the other retail trade and service sector industries, the establishment sales size test in 1978 was annual sales of $250,000 or less (this became $275,000 on July 1, 1978). These industries include 607–38, 647–98, 749–78, 787–837, 839, 847, 878, and 879.

For industries in which partial, by size class, coverage exists, the probability of coverage was calculated from knowledge of the fraction of employees in an industry who were employed in establishments with sales or receipts greater than $250,000 in 1977. The *1977 Census of Retail Trade* and the *1977 Census of Selected Service Industries* contained data on the number of employees by sales class and industry (U.S., Bureau of the Census 1980a and 1980b). Unfortunately, the data was not available for many census three-digit industries in the service sector, and these were excluded from the analyses. While the size-class breaks in the published census volumes occurred at $100,000 and $300,000, the Bureau of the Census prepared for this study unpublished tabulations of the number of employees employed in each industry in establishments with annual sales in the $100,000 to $250,000 range. This permitted the computation of the probability that workers in each of the remaining retail trade and service industries were covered by the overtime pay provisions of the FLSA. These probabilities are reported in table 5.4 in the text.

6. *Section 13a(3)—Seasonal Amusement or Recreation Establishments*
It is not possible to separate seasonal establishments. Hence, it was necessary for us to exclude all individuals in industry 809 from the sample.

7. *Section 13a(4)—Custom Manufacturing in Exempt Retail Trade*
This is a minor category; it is covered by the general retail trade treatment.

8. *Section 13a(5)—Catching and Processing Fish and Seafood Section 13a(6)—Agriculture*
Exclude individuals with industry codes 017 to 028 from the sample.

9. *Section 13a(8)—Small Newspapers with Circulations Less than 4,000*
To be conservative, observations were excluded from the sample if industry code 338 and the individual did not reside in a standard metropolitan statistical area (SMSA).

10. *Section 13a(10)—Switchboard Operators of Small Telephone Exchanges*
To be conservative, individuals were excluded from the sample if they had occupation code 385 and industry code 448 and they did not reside in an SMSA.

11. *Section 13a(12)—Seamen on Foreign Vessels*
    See Section 13b(6) rule.

12. *Section 13a(15)—Babysitters Employed on a Casual Basis*
    This is primarily a minimum wage exemption. It is unlikely that any individuals in this category would work overtime, so no exclusions were made here.

13. *Section (7i)—Commission Salesworkers in Retail Trade or Service Establishments*
    Since it was not possible to identify who gets paid on commission all salesworkers in these industries (occupation codes 283, 284) were excluded. This was subsumed in the general salesperson exclusion above.

14. *Section 13b(1)—Motor Carriers*
    Exclude individuals with industry codes 417 from the sample.

15. *Section 13b(2)—Railroads*
    Exclude individuals with industry code 407 from the sample.

16. *Section 13b(3)—Air Transport*
    Exclude individuals with industry code 427 from the sample.

17. *Section 13b(6)—Seamen*
    Exclude individuals with occupation code 661 and industry code 419 from the sample.

18. *Section 13b(8)—(1977 Amendments) Employees of Hotels, Motels, and Restaurants, except Maids and Custodians. Maids and Custodians Covered after 40 hours, all others after 44*
    If the industry code for an individual was 669, 777, or 778 and the occupation code was *not* 901, 902, or 903, then the individual was placed in the "probability" sample if his or her hours of work were more than 44. For occupation codes 901, 902, and 903, the individual was placed in the "probability" sample.

19. *Section 13b(9)—Announcers, Newseditors, and Chief Engineers in Small Radio or TV Stations*
    The restriction here is on the size of the broadcast area.

To be safe, all individuals *not* residing in SMSAs were excluded; that is, *if* an individual's industry code was 447 *and* occupation code was *184* or *193*, the individual was excluded if he or she did not reside in an SMSA.

20. *Section 13b(10)—Salesmen, Partsmen, and Mechanics of Autos, Trucks, Farm Implements, Trailers, Boats and Aircraft*
Exclude individuals whose industry code is 639, 647, 648, or 649 and whose occupation code is 260, 261, 262, 471, 472, 473, 474, 480, or 481.

21. *Section 13b(11)—Drivers Paid on Trip Basis*
Less than 10,000 individuals are exempted here, so this exclusion is ignored.

22. *Section 13b(2)—Agriculture and Irrigation*
Included with Section 13a(6) exemption above.

23. *Section 13b(13)—Farmworkers in Livestock Auctions*
Section 13b(14)—Country Elevators in Areas of Production
Section 13b(15)—Processing Maple Sap
Cannot identify because of small number, these are ignored.

24. *Section 13b(16)—Transportation of Farm Products*
Exclude individuals if their occupation code was 715 and their industry code was 018. This is included with the Section 13a(5)(6) exemptions above.

25. *Section 13b(17)—Taxicab Drivers*
Exclude individuals with occupation code 714.

26. *Section 13b(21)—Domestic Service Live-Ins*
Exclude individuals with occupation codes 980 to 984.

27. *Section 13b(24)—Substitute Parents for Institutionalized Children*
Too small a category to be concerned about.

28. *Section 13b(27)—Motion Picture Theaters*
Exclude individuals with industry code 807.

29. *Section 13b(28)—Small Loggers (less than 9 employees)*
To be conservative, all individuals in industry code 107 were excluded.

30. *Section 7b(3)—Independent Bulk Petroleum Dealers*
The exclusion here occurs if gross sales are less than $1 million *and* applies for less than 12 hours a day or 56 hours a week. Thus, for individuals with industry code 558, if weekly hours were greater than 56, the probability of coverage was set equal to 1. If weekly hours were less than 56, they are excluded from the sample.

31. *Section 7k—Federal Fire Protection ane Law Enforcement Officials*
Exclude if individuals were in industry 917 and occupation codes 961 through 965.

32. *Section 7m—Tobacco Handling and Processing Incidental to Auction Sales*
Section 13b(29)—Concessions in National Parks
Section 13h—Cotton and Sugar Service Employees
Section 13i—Cotton Ginning
Section 13j—Processing Sugar Beets, Molasses or Cane
Section 13b(29) exemptions were included in the seasonal amusement exemption (item 6). The others fall within the agriculture services sector exemption, which is included in item 8 above.

33. *Section 7j—Hospitals and Nursing Homes*
Premium goes into effect after 8 hours a day or 80 hours per 14-day period. This is a large category (2.8 million workers). They were included in the analysis if they worked more than 40 hours in the survey week since only survey week hours were reported; that is, it was assured that the survey week hours were not atypical.

Finally, note that all self-employed individuals were excluded from the samples.

D · DETAILS OF NONCOMPLIANCE ESTIMATES

TABLE D.1

Probit Analysis of Noncompliance:
Complete Coverage Sample, 1978
(absolute value asymptotic *t*-statistics in parentheses)

	(1)	(2)	(3)	(4)
CONST	−.769 (2.8)	−.747 (2.6)	−.693 (2.4)	−.679 (2.3)
Z1	.006 (2.2)	.006 (2.2)	.005 (1.9)	.005 (1.9)
Z2	.065 (0.7)	.066 (0.7)	.111 (1.2)	.111 (1.2)
Z3	.022 (0.3)	−.021 (0.3)	−.022 (0.3)	−.023 (0.3)
Z4	.147 (1.3)	.146 (1.3)	.094 (0.8)	.092 (0.8)
Z5	.157 (0.5)	.173 (0.6)	.246 (0.8)	.265 (0.9)
Z6	.007 (0.0)	.010 (0.1)	.059 (0.4)	.063 (0.4)
Z7	−.006 (0.4)	−.006 (0.4)	−.007 (0.4)	−.007 (0.4)
Z8	−.018 (0.2)	−.165 (0.2)	.005 (0.1)	.008 (0.1)
Z9	−.057 (0.7)	−.057 (0.7)	−.065 (0.8)	−.063 (0.8)
Z10[a]	−.016 (4.3)	−.016 (4.3)	−.015 (3.9)	−.015 (3.9)
Z11	−.207 (1.5)	−.207 (1.5)	−.205 (1.4)	−.203 (1.4)
Z12	−.449 (5.8)	−.452 (5.8)	−.364 (4.5)	−.367 (4.5)
Z13	.402 (3.0)	.401 (3.0)		
Z14	.121 (0.7)	.122 (0.7)	.030 (0.2)	.031 (0.2)
Z15	.336 (2.6)	.336 (2.6)	.268 (1.9)	.268 (1.9)
Z16	−.378 (3.2)	−.378 (3.2)	−.458 (3.6)	−.457 (3.6)
Z17	−.551 (4.2)	−.550 (4.2)	−.622 (4.5)	−.622 (4.5)
Z18	−.110 (0.7)	−.109 (0.7)	−.294 (1.5)	−.293 (1.5)
Z19	−.106 (0.7)	−.106 (0.7)	−.168 (1.0)	−.168 (1.0)
Z20	−.056 (0.2)	−.056 (0.2)	−.087 (0.4)	−.087 (0.4)
Z21	−74.868 (0.8)		−92.134 (0.9)	
Z22		−.181 (0.8)		−.201 (0.8)
L	−1028.0	−1028.0	−921.2	−921.2
L*	−923.9	−923.9	−840.8	−840.8
N/n	.097/3,231	.097/3,231	.090/3,046	.090/3,046

Source: May 1978 *CPS*.
Notes: (1)(2) restricted to employees who report being paid by the hour, individuals said to be in noncompliance if they receive *no* premium pay for overtime
     (3)(4) same as (1) and (2) but restricted to private employees
     Z1   age
     Z2   1 = male; 0 = female
     Z3   1 = married, spouse present; 0 = other
     Z4   1 = black; 0 = other
     Z5   1 = other nonwhite; 0 = other
     Z6   1 = Hispanic; 0 = other
     Z7   Years of schooling completed
     Z8   1 = reside in central city of SMSA; 0 = otherwise
     Z9   1 = reside in SMSA outside of central city; 0 = other
     Z10 usual weekly earnings if reported; 0 = otherwise
     Z11 1 = usual weekly earnings not reported; 0 = otherwise
     Z12 1 = union member or covered by union contract; 0 = otherwise

TABLE D.1 (*continued*)

Z13	1 = government employee; 0 = otherwise
Z14	1 = mining; 0 = otherwise
Z15	1 = construction; 0 = otherwise
Z16	1 = durable manufacturing; 0 = otherwise
Z17	1 = nondurable manufacturing; 0 = otherwise
Z18	1 = transportation and public utilities; 0 = otherwise
Z19	1 = wholesale trade; 0 = otherwise
Z20	1 = finance, insurance, and real estate; 0 = otherwise
Z21	Total number of FLSA compliance actions in the state in 1978/total number of private and federal nonsupervisory employees in the state in 1978
Z22	Total FLSA compliance budget in the state in 1978/total number of private and federal nonsupervisory employees in the state in 1978
L	Log of likelihood for binomial model
L^*	Log of likelihood function for full model at convergence
N	Proportion of sample in noncompliance
n	Sample size
a	Coefficient has been multiplied by 10.

TABLE D.2

Probit Analysis of Noncompliance:
Complete Coverage Sample, 1977
(absolute value *t*-statistics in parentheses)

	(1)	(2)
Z1	.064 (1.4)	.071 (1.3)
Z2	1.276 (1.1)	.561 (0.4)
Z3	1.542 (1.7)	1.569 (1.5)
Z4	1.901 (2.1)	2.286 (2.2)
Z7	.010 (0.7)	−.114 (0.6)
Z'10	.001 (0.1)	.007 (0.1)
Z12	−1.191 (1.6)	−1.426 (1.6)
Z14	−9.028 (0.0)	−9.163 (0.0)
Z15	−.737 (0.7)	−.595 (0.4)
Z16	−1.593 (1.4)	−1.542 (1.2)
Z17	−1.545 (1.3)	−2.223 (1.7)
Z18	−1.544 (1.3)	−1.274 (1.0)
Z19	−10.062 (0.0)	−10.657 (0.0)
Z20	1.132 (0.6)	.891 (0.5)
Z13	−6.983 (0.0)	−7.436 (0.0)
Z23	.042 (0.3)	−.071 (0.4)
L	−30.27	−28.55
L*	−17.66	−14.93
N/n	.159/69	.145/69

Source: *QES*

Notes: See table D.1 for table notes and variable definitions. All variables are defined as before
save

Z'10   Straight-time hourly earnings
Z23   Establishment size
(1)   Noncompliance = failure to receive a premium of at least time and a half
(2)   Noncompliance = failure to receive a premium of at least 1.4 straight-time hourly
        wages

TABLE D.3
OLS Noncompliance Regressions:
Partial Coverage
Sample, 1978
(absolute value t-statistics in parentheses)

Variable	(1)	(2)	(3)	(4)	(5)	(6)
CONST	.642 (7.5)	.643 (7.5)	.643 (7.5)	-.614 (0.9)	-.619 (0.9)	-.607 (0.8)
Z1				.017 (2.6)	.018 (2.7)	.018 (2.7)
Z2				.014 (0.1)	.013 (0.1)	.012 (0.1)
Z3				-.344 (1.9)	-.357 (2.0)	-.356 (1.9)
Z4 + Z5				-.031 (0.1)	-.020 (0.01)	-.029 (0.1)
Z6				-.437 (1.1)	-.438 (1.1)	-.423 (1.0)
Z7				.082 (1.8)	.081 (1.7)	.080 (1.7)
Z10[a]				-.012 (1.2)	-.013 (1.2)	-.013 (1.2)
Z11				-.225 (0.6)	-.247 (0.7)	-.240 (0.6)
Z12				-.336 (1.2)	-.333 (1.2)	-.333 (1.2)
C	-.440 (3.9)	-.447 (3.5)	-.457 (3.4)	1.295 (1.4)	1.388 (1.5)	1.392 (1.5)
C^2						
C*Z1				-.021 (2.4)	-.022 (2.5)	-.021 (2.5)
C*Z2				.015 (0.1)	.016 (0.1)	.016 (0.1)
C*Z3				.305 (1.3)	.325 (1.4)	.323 (1.4)
C*(Z4 + Z5)				.607 (0.1)	.053 (0.1)	.072 (0.2)
C*Z6				.549 (1.1)	.567 (1.1)	.554 (1.1)
C*Z7				-.090 (1.5)	-.089 (1.5)	-.089 (1.5)
C*Z10[a]				-.002 (0.1)	.001 (0.1)	-.002 (0.1)
C*Z11				-.018 (0.0)	-.002 (0.0)	-.010 (0.0)
C*Z12				.272 (0.8)	-.249 (0.7)	.246 (0.7)
C*Z21		7.546 (0.1)			-82.028 (1.3)	
C*Z22			.033 (0.2)			-.197 (1.2)
R^2	.028	.028	.028	.136	.139	.139

Source: May 1978 *CPS*.
Notes: See table D.1 for variable definitions. All variables are defined as before save C, which is the estimated proportion of employees in the industry subject to the overtime pay provisions of the FLSA (see table 5.4).
Noncompliance was defined as failure to receive any premium pay for hours in excess of 40 per week.
[a]Coefficient multiplied by 10.
n = 535 for all equations.

TABLE D.4
OLS Noncompliance Regressions:
Partial Coverage Sample, 1978
(absolute value t-statistics in parentheses)

Variable	(1)	(2)	(3)	(4)	(5)	(6)
CONST	−.013 (0.1)	−.013 (0.1)	−.012 (0.0)	−1.710 (2.2)	−1.701 (2.2)	−1.693 (2.2)
$Z1$				.021 (3.1)	.021 (3.1)	.021 (3.1)
$Z2$				.005 (0.0)	.004 (0.0)	.003 (0.0)
$Z3$				−.420 (2.3)	−.430 (2.4)	−.429 (2.4)
$Z4 + Z5$				−.225 (0.6)	−.212 (0.6)	−.221 (0.6)
$Z6$				−.314 (0.8)	−.317 (0.8)	−.303 (0.7)
$Z7$				.109 (2.3)	.109 (2.3)	.108 (2.3)
$Z10^a$				−.018 (1.7)	−.018 (1.7)	−.018 (1.7)
$Z11$				−.373 (1.0)	−.391 (1.0)	−.385 (1.0)
$Z12$				−.337 (1.2)	−.334 (1.2)	−.334 (1.2)
C	1.650 (2.2)	1.643 (2.2)	1.635 (2.2)	4.143 (3.3)	4.192 (3.3)	4.207 (3.3)
C^2	−1.537 (2.9)	−1.537 (2.9)	−1.536 (2.9)	−1.885 (3.4)	−1.861 (3.3)	−1.867 (3.3)
$C*Z1$				−.025 (2.9)	−.025 (2.9)	−.025 (2.9)
$C*Z2$				.030 (0.1)	.031 (0.1)	.031 (0.1)
$C*Z3$				.408 (1.7)	.425 (1.8)	.424 (1.8)
$C*(Z4 + Z5)$				.312 (0.7)	.296 (0.6)	.314 (0.7)
$C*Z6$				.440 (0.9)	.458 (0.9)	.445 (0.9)
$C*Z7$				−.120 (2.0)	−.119 (2.0)	−.119 (2.0)
$C*Z10^a$				.008 (0.6)	.008 (0.6)	.008 (0.6)
$C*Z11$				.163 (0.3)	.175 (0.4)	.168 (0.3)
$C*Z12$				.308 (0.9)	.287 (0.9)	.284 (0.9)
$C*Z21$		6.688 (0.1)			−74.784 (1.2)	
$C*Z22$			.028 (0.2)			−.183 (1.2)
R^2	.043	.043	.043	.155	.157	.157

Source: May 1978 CPS.

Notes: See table D.1 for variable definitions and table D.3 for notes.

n = 535 for all equations.

TABLE D.5

Implied Partial Derivatives,
OLS Noncompliance Results:
Partially Covered Sample

		Variable	$\partial P_C/\partial Z$
−+	Z1	age	−.003 (1.3)
?	Z2	sex (1 = male)	.029 (0.4)
?	Z4 + Z5	race (1 = nonwhite)	.036 (0.3)
+	Z6	Hispanic (1 = yes)	.112 (0.7)
−	Z7	education	−.008 (0.4)
−	Z10[a]	earnings	−.011 (2.3)
−	Z12	union	−.064 (0.8)

Source: Derived from the estimates in column (4) of table D.3.

E · A MODEL OF DEMAND AND SUPPLY OF MANDATORY OVERTIME PROVISIONS

An employee's willingness to be employed in an establishment in which he or she would be required to work mandatory overtime is undoubtedly positively related to the wage premium d_i the employee would receive for such a working condition. This willingness is also undoubtedly related to a vector of personal characteristics and characteristics of the employer that influence the employee's desire to regularly work long workweeks, $\mathbf{Y_r}$. For example, older employees, employees with responsibilities at home, and employees working in firms with unpleasant working conditions might, other things being equal, prefer not to be required to work mandatory overtime.

Without loss of generality, a model of these relations can be constructed by assuming that an individual's willingness to work mandatory overtime can be expressed by

$$S_{1i}^* = \gamma_{10}d_i + \sum_{r=1}^{R} \gamma_{1r}Y_{ri} + V_{1i} \qquad \gamma_{10} > 0$$

$$S_{1i} = 1 \text{ if } S_{1i}^* > 0$$
$$= 0 \text{ otherwise.} \qquad\qquad (E.1)$$

Here V_{1i} is a random error term and S_{1i}^* is an unobserved variable that represents the individual's willingness to be employed in a firm requiring mandatory overtime. Although S_{1i}^* is not observed, its cutoff value can be arbitrarily scaled to be 0, so that if S_{1i}^* is greater than 0, the individual would choose to be employed by a firm that requires mandatory overtime: $S_{1i} = 1$. Similarly, if the index is less than or equal to 0, the individual would choose to be employed at a firm where overtime is voluntary: $S_{1i} = 0$.

Turning next to the employer side of the market, an employer's willingness to have an employee be subject to mandatory overtime provisions is undoubtedly negatively related to the wage premium d_i the employer would have to pay the individual to induce him or her to accept such a working condition. The employer's demand for the provision is also related to a vector of characteristics of the employee and of the firm that influence the net benefits of having mandatory overtime provisions Z_m. For example, an employer operating a firm in a continuous process industry might perceive it to be important to have mandatory overtime provisions. Similarly, an employer might believe it more important to have such provisions for skilled production workers, whose absence might create a bottleneck, than for unskilled clerical workers.

Again, without loss of generality a model of this can be constructed by assuming that the employer's demand for mandatory overtime provisions for individual i is given by

$$S_{2i}^* = \gamma_{20}d_i + \sum_{m=1}^{M} \gamma_{2m}Z_{mi} + V_{2i}, \qquad \gamma_{20} < 0$$

$$S_{2i} = 1 \text{ if } S_{2i}^* > 0$$
$$= 0 \text{ otherwise.} \qquad\qquad\qquad (\text{E.2})$$

Once again, V_{2i} is a random error term, and S_{2i}^* is an unobserved variable that represents the employer's preference for having individual i subject to a mandatory overtime provision. This index can be scaled so that when it exceeds 0 the employer demands a mandatory overtime provision for individual i: $S_{2i} = 1$. Otherwise the employer does not: $S_{2i} = 0$. Under the appropriate assumptions about the error terms (joint normally distributed), the choice model in E.1 and E.2 corresponds to a bivariate probit model (estimation of such a model is described in Heckman 1978).

It should be stressed, however, that the choices S_{1i} and S_{2i} are only partially observed. In particular, the only thing that can be observed is whether an individual actually is employed by a firm requiring mandatory overtime. Suppose that labor markets are sufficiently competitive so that an employee will accept a position requiring mandatory overtime only if it is in his or her best interests to do so, $S_{1i} = 1$, and that an employer will offer such a position only if it is in his or her best interests, $S_{2i} = 1$. It immediately follows that the outcomes produced by the market can be represented by a single binary random variable

$$S_{3i} = S_{1i}S_{2i} \tag{E.3}$$

whose distribution is given (see Poirer 1980) by

$$P_i = P_r(S_{3i} = 1) = P_r(S_{1i} = 1 \text{ and } S_{2i} = 1)$$

$$= F(\gamma_{10}d_i + \sum_{r=1}^{R} \gamma_{1r}Y_{ri}, \gamma_{20}d_i + \sum_{m=1}^{M} \gamma_{2m}Z_{mi}; \rho)$$

$$1 - P_i = P_r(S_{3i} = 0) = P_r(S_{1i} = 0 \text{ or } S_{2i} = 0)$$

$$= 1 - F(\;) . \tag{E.4}$$

Here the variances of V_1 and V_2 have been normalized to equal unity; ρ is the correlation between these two error terms, and F denotes the bivariate standard normal distribution.

Software limitations have so far prevented the estimation of this complete model, (7.1 to 7.3, E.1 to E.4), either by maximum likelihood methods or by an iterative approach that leads to consistent estimates. Rather, it has been assumed that the structural choice model embedded in E.1 to E.4 can be approximated by

$$S_{3i}^* = \delta_0 d_i + \sum_{r=1}^{R} \delta_r Y_{ri} + \sum_{m=1}^{M} \delta_{R+m} Z_{mi} + \mu_i$$

$$S_{3i} = 1 \text{ if } S_{3i}^* > 0$$

$$= 0 \text{ otherwise} \tag{E.5}$$

where S^*_{3i} is again an unobservable variable and μ_i a random error term. That is, it has been assumed that the employer and employee choice functions can be approximated by a single market decision rule.

Consistent estimates of the model specified in 7.1, 7.2, 7.3, and E.5 can be obtained using an iterative procedure originally suggested by Lung-fei Lee (1978).[1] One can substitute the wage equa-

---

1. One must caution, however, that because the true sample selection rule has only been approximated with a univariate probit model, the statistical properties of the estimates of equations 7.2 and 7.3 when controlled for selectivity bias are not obvious. More precisely, their consistency is conditional on equation E.5 being the correct underlying selection rule (see Poirer 1980).

tions 7.2 and 7.3 into 7.1 and E.5 to obtain a reduced form probit selection model

$$S_{3i}^* = \sum_{t=1}^{T} B_t X_{ti}^* + n_i \tag{E.6}$$

where the X^*_{ti} are all the predetermined variables in the model (X, Y, and Zs) and n_i is a random error term. Now suppose that the error terms from this reduced form selection model and the wage equations are jointly normally distributed with means and covariances given by

$$\begin{bmatrix} \varepsilon_{im} \\ \varepsilon_{iv} \\ n_i \end{bmatrix} \sim N \left(\begin{bmatrix} 0 \\ 0 \\ 0 \end{bmatrix}, \begin{bmatrix} \sigma_{mm} & \sigma_{mv} & \sigma_{mn} \\ \sigma_{vm} & \sigma_{vv} & \sigma_{vn} \\ \sigma_{nm} & \sigma_{nv} & \sigma_{nn} \end{bmatrix} \right). \tag{E.7}$$

Under these assumptions one can show that

$$E(\log W_{im}|X_{ji}, S_{3i} = 1) = \sum_{j=1}^{K} \alpha_{jm} X_{ji} + (\sigma_{mn}/\sigma_n)\lambda_{im} + h_{im} \tag{E.8}$$

$$E(\log W_{iv}|X_{ji}, S_{3i} = 0) = \sum_{j=1}^{K} \alpha_{jv} X_{ji} + (\sigma_{vn}/\sigma_n)\lambda_{iv} + h_{iv}. \tag{E.9}$$

Here the h_i are normally distributed random variables with mean 0 and the λ_i are given by

$$\lambda_{im} = \phi\left(\sum_{t=1}^{T} (B_t/\sigma_n)X_{ti}^* \right) \bigg/ \Phi\left(\sum_{t=1}^{T} (B_t/\sigma_n)X_{ti}^* \right)$$

$$\lambda_{iv} = -\phi\left(\sum_{t=1}^{T} (B_t/\sigma_n)X_{ti}^* \right) \bigg/ \left[1 - \Phi\left(\sum_{t=1}^{T} (B_t/\sigma_n)X_{ti}^* \right) \right] \tag{E.10}$$

where ϕ denotes the normal probability density function and Φ the corresponding distribution function (see Johnson and Kotz 1972).

Equations E.8 and E.9 make it clear why OLS estimates of the underlying wage equations 7.2 and 7.3 may lead to biased estimates. As long as the error terms in the wage equations are correlated with the error term in the reduced form selection rule, $\sigma_{mn} \neq 0$, $\sigma_{vn} \neq 0$,

OLS estimates will be biased because of an omitted variable. While λ_{im} and λ_{iv} are not directly observed, estimates of them may be obtained by first estimating the reduced form probit selection model E.6, obtaining estimated coefficients, $\hat{B}_l/\sigma_n$, and then using these estimates to compute predicted values $\hat{\lambda}_{im}$ and $\hat{\lambda}_{iv}$ for each individual. Lee (1978) shows that estimation of 7.2 (7.3) by OLS, with $\hat{\lambda}_{im}$ ($\hat{\lambda}_{iv}$) added as an additional explanatory variable, over a sample of individuals who are (are not) required to work mandatory overtime, will lead to consistent estimates of the α_{jm} (α_{jv}). Consequently, consistent estimates of the estimated wage differential associated with being required to work mandatory overtime may be obtained.

F · DETAILS OF COMPUTATION OF COMPENSATING WAGE DIFFERENTIALS

TABLE F.1

OLS and Selectivity Adjusted Estimates of
the Wage Equations Used in the Computation of
the Compensating Wage Differentials

| | Log Wage Equations | | | | |
| | OLS | | Selectivity Bias Corrected | | |
Variable	Mandatory Sector	Voluntary Sector	Mandatory Sector	Voluntary Sector	Probit
X_1	.040 (4.4)	.028 (6.7)	.039 (3.4)	−.030 (5.0)	−.018 (1.0)
X_2	−.682 (3.6)	−.519 (5.8)	−.651 (2.7)	−.562 (4.3)	.383 (1.1)
X_3	−.007 (0.6)	.040 (6.2)	−.008 (0.5)	.035 (3.8)	.027 (1.1)
X_4	.363 (0.7)	−1.192 (4.6)	.414 (0.7)	−.958 (2.6)	−1.300 (1.4)
X_5	.078 (9.6)	.053 (13.3)	.084 (7.8)	.060 (9.9)	−.052 (3.3)
X_6	.007 (0.2)	.016 (1.0)	.019 (0.4)	.023 (1.1)	−.061 (1.0)
X_7	.016 (0.2)	−.136 (3.2)	.037 (0.3)	−.121 (2.0)	−.109 (0.6)
X_8	.327 (6.2)	.202 (6.9)	.305 (4.5)	.159 (3.6)	.214 (2.0)
X_9	−.282 (4.5)	−.364 (12.6)	−.198 (2.2)	−.299 (6.5)	−.313 (2.6)
X_{10}	−.096 (1.4)	−.109 (2.6)	−.143 (1.6)	−.130 (2.1)	.187 (1.3)
X_{11}	.068 (1.1)	.015 (0.5)	.093 (1.2)	.040 (0.9)	−.214 (2.0)
X_{12}					−.311 (1.5)
X_{13}					.013 (1.3)
X_{14}					.242 (0.6)
X_{15}					.033 (1.0)
X_{16}					−4.494 (0.0)
X_{17}					.048 (6.2)
X_{18}					.058 (0.5)
X_{19}					−4.736 (0.0)
X_{20}					−.143 (1.4)
X_{21}					.046 (1.2)
X_{22}					−.004 (0.6)
X_{23}					−.177 (0.9)
CONST	.265 (2.1)	.654 (9.6)	.453 (2.4)	.420 (3.4)	−.279 (1.0)
λ			−.204 (1.8)	−.454 (2.9)	
R^2	.633	.474	.648	.486	
Chi-squared/log likelihood					109.9/−411.4
n	165	943	165	943	1108

Source: 1977 *QES*.

Notes: Numbers in parentheses are the absolute values of t-ratios for OLS models, absolute values of corrected t-ratios for model corrected for selectivity bias, and absolute value of asymptotic t-ratios for the probit model.

TABLE F.1 (*continued*)

X_1	Total years of labor market experience
X_2	X_1 squared/1000
X_3	Total years of experience with current employer
X_4	X_3 squared/1000
X_5	Years of formal school
X_6	Years of trade school
X_7	1 = health limits work; 0 = otherwise
X_8	1 = union member or covered by union contract; 0 = otherwise
X_9	1 = female; 0 = male
X_{10}	1 = nonwhite; 0 = white
X_{11}	1 = married, spouse present; 0 = otherwise
X_{12}	1 = employee has a second job; 0 = otherwise
X_{13}	Hours of work on second job if reported; 0 = otherwise
X_{14}	1 = hours of second job not reported; 0 = otherwise
X_{15}	Size of establishment (number of employees/1000) if reported; 0 = otherwise
X_{16}	1 = size of establishment not reported; 0 = otherwise
X_{17}	Weekly overtime hours
X_{18}	Travel time to work if reported; 0 = otherwise
X_{19}	1 = travel time not reported; 0 = otherwise
X_{20}	1 = respondent feels comfort on the job is "okay"; 0 = otherwise
X_{21}	Number of dependents excluding spouse
X_{22}	Other family members' earnings/1000 if reported; 0 = otherwise
X_{23}	1 = other family members' earnings not reported; 0 = otherwise
CONST	Constant term
λ	Estimated value of the inverse of the Mills ratio

G · A MODEL TO ESTIMATE FULLY COMPENSATING WAGE DIFFERENTIALS

Suppose that the individual's utility function in figure 7.1 is any monotonic transformation of the Cobb-Douglas function

$$U = Y^{\alpha}L^{1-\alpha}. \tag{G.1}$$

If α were known, one could compute the level of utility achieved by a representative individual who was required to work mandatory overtime from

$$U_1 = Y_1{}^{\alpha}L_1{}^{1-\alpha} \tag{G.2}$$

where

$$Y_1 = W_1\bar{H} + W_1(1.5)(H_1 - \bar{H}) + M$$
$$L_1 = T - H_1.$$

Here W_1 is the individual's observed wage, H_1 the individual's observed weekly hours of work, M the individual's weekly nonlabor income, $\bar{H}$ the number of hours after which the overtime premium goes into effect (typically forty), and T the total number of hours in a week or 168.

Given the utility function specified in G.2, if the individual was employed by a firm that did not require mandatory overtime he or she would work H_0 hours, where H_0 is given by

$$H_0 = \alpha T + (\alpha - 1)(M - .5W_0\bar{H})/W_0(1.5) \quad \text{if } H_0 > \bar{H}$$
$$= \alpha T + (\alpha - 1)(M/W_0) \quad \text{if } H_0 \leq \bar{H}. \tag{G.3}$$

G.3 represents the labor supply curve for individuals in the nonmandatory overtime sector. W_0 is not observed for individuals employed in the mandatory overtime sector, rather W_1, which equals $W_0(1 + d)$ is. Hence, G.3 can be written

$$H_0 = \alpha T + (\alpha - 1)(M - .5(W_1/(1 + d))$$
$$\times \bar{H})/(W_1/(1 + d))(1.5) \qquad \text{if } H_0 > \bar{H}$$
$$= \alpha T + (\alpha - 1)(M(1 + d)/W_1) \qquad \text{if } H_0 \leq \bar{H} . \qquad (G.4)$$

Observe that given α, everything on the right-hand side of G.4 is known save for d. Moreover, for each value of d, there will exist a corresponding value of H_0 and hence Y_0. Thus, the individual's utility from being employed by a firm in which mandatory overtime is not required can be specified by

$$U_0(d) = (Y_0(d))^\alpha (L_0(d))^{1-\alpha} \qquad (G.5)$$

One can then set G.5 equal to G.2 and solve for d^*. This will be the fully compensating straight-time wage differential for mandatory overtime; it can be contrasted to the actual differentials that have been estimated.

Of course, to proceed along this line first requires an estimate of α, and it is natural to obtain such an estimate from the sample of people who are employed by firms that do not require mandatory overtime. For this sample of 943 individuals a labor supply function is estimated in the form of

$$H_i = \alpha T + (\alpha - 1)Q_i + \epsilon_i \qquad (G.6)$$

where

$$Q = (M - .5W\bar{H})/1.5W \qquad \text{if } H > \bar{H}$$
$$= M/W \qquad \text{if } H \leq \bar{H} .$$

Estimation of equation G.6 yields an estimate of α of 0.224, with an estimated standard error of 0.001.[1]

---

1. Variants of equation G.6 in which α was specified to be a linear function of each individual's sex (0,1), race (0,1), marital status (0,1), health status (0,1) and number of dependents were also estimated. When evaluated at the mean values of these variables for individuals employed by firms that *required* mandatory overtime, the resulting estimate of α was almost identical (0.223) to the value reported in the text.

These estimates imply that the marginal propensity to consume out of unearned income is less than one-quarter, a result that is much smaller than other investigators have found. In future work the authors therefore hope to test the sensitivity of these results to alternative functional forms. For now, the estimate of the

With this estimate in hand, U_1 can be computed, using G.2 and the mean values of the variables for individuals employed by firms requiring mandatory overtime.[2] Similarly, H_0 and U_0, conditional upon d, can be computed from G.4 and G.5. Finally, equating U_0 to U_1 and solving the resulting nonlinear equation for d, yields the estimate of the fully compensating straight-time wage differential for mandatory overtime. The data suggest that this is approximately 1.1 percent.

---

fully compensating differential must be taken to be quite preliminary. It should be stressed, however, that if α were larger, the estimate of the fully compensating differentials would be even smaller.

2. The parameters used in this simulation are $T = 168$, $W_1 = \$6.026$, $H_1 = 45.139$, $\bar{H} = 40$, and $M = \$80.615$. Note that in the data, M represents all family income except for the respondent's labor earnings; this includes labor earnings of other family members. The data unfortunately did not permit the computation of family nonlabor income, which is theoretically the more appropriate variable to use, unless the respondent's labor supply is conditional on other family members' labor supply decisions.

REFERENCES

Abowd, John, and Ashenfelter, Orley.
    1979. "Unemployment and Compensating Wage Differentials." Princeton University Industrial Relations Section Working Paper No. 120.

Abowd, John, and Farber, Henry.
    1978. "Relative Wages, Union Membership and Job Queues: Econometric Evidence Based on Panel Data." Mimeographed. Princeton University Industrial Relations Section.

Ashenfelter, Orley, and Smith, Robert S.
    1979. "Compliance with the Minimum Wage Law." *Journal of Political Economy* 87, 2 (April 1979).

Becker, Gary.
    1964. *Human Capital.* New York: Columbia University Press.

Brown, Charles, and Medoff, James.
    1978. "Trade Unions in the Production Process." *Journal of Political Economy* 86, 3 (June 1978).

Brown, Scott.
    1978. "Moonlighting Increases Sharply in 1977." *Monthly Labor Review* 101, 1 (January 1978).

Cahill, Marion.
    1932. *Shorter Hours.* New York: Columbia University Press.

Carstensen, Larry, and Woltman, Henry.
    1979. "Comparing Earnings Data from the CPS and Em-

ployers' Records." Paper presented at the 1979 annual meetings of the American Statistical Association.

Clark, Kim.
1980.   "The Impact of Unionization on Productivity: A Case Study." *Industrial and Labor Relations Review* 33, 4 (July 1980).

Commons, John R., and Andrews, John B.
1920.   *Principles of Labor Legislation.* New York: Harper and Brothers.

Connell, John F.
1979.   "Multiple Job Holding and Marginal Tax Rates." *National Tax Journal* 32, 1 (March 1979).

Duncan, Greg.
1976.   "Earnings Functions and Nonpecuniary Benefits." *Journal of Human Resources* 11, 4 (Fall 1976).

Duncan, Greg, and Stafford, Frank.
1980.   "Do Union Members Receive Compensating Wage Differentials?" *American Economic Review* 70, 3 (June 1980).

Ehrenberg, Ronald G.
1971a. *Fringe Benefits and Overtime Behavior.* Lexington, Mass.: D. C. Heath.
1971b. "Heterogeneous Labor, the Internal Labor Market and the Employment-Hours Decision." *Journal of Economic Theory* 3,1 (March 1971).
1971c. "The Impact of the Overtime Premium on Employment Hours in U.S. Industry." *Western Economic Journal* 9, 2 (June 1971).
1980.   "Retirement System Characteristics and Compensating Wage Differentials in the Public Sector." *Industrial and Labor Relations Review* 33, 4 (July 1980).

Eisner, Robert.
1978.   "Employment Taxes and Subsidies." In *Work Time and Employment.* Special Report No. 28. Washington, D.C.: National Commission for Employment Policy.

Freeman, Richard.
1978.   "The Effect of Unionism on Fringe Benefits." NBER Working Paper No. 280. Cambridge, Mass.

Freeman, Richard, and Medoff, James.
1979.   "The Two Faces of Unionism." *Public Interest,* no. 57 (Fall 1979).

Gramlich, Edward.
    1976.   "Impact of Minimum Wages on Other Wages, Employment and Family Incomes." *Brookings Papers on Economic Activity 1976-2*. Washington, D.C.: Brookings Institution.

Gramlich, Edward, and Wolkoff, M. J.
    1979.   "A Procedure for Evaluating Income Distribution Policies." *Journal of Human Resources* 14, 3 (Summer 1979).

Grossman, Jonathan.
    1978.   "Fair Labor Standards Act of 1938: Maximum Struggle for a Minimum Wage." *Monthly Labor Review* 101, 6 (June 1978).

Hamermesh, Daniel.
    1976.   "Econometric Studies of Labor Demand and Their Application to Policy Analysis." *Journal of Human Resources* 11, 4 (Fall 1976).

Hamermesh, Daniel, and Grant, James.
    1979.   "Econometric Studies of Labor-Labor Substitution and Their Implications for Policy." *Journal of Human Resources* 14, 4 (Fall 1979).

Heckman, James.
    1978.   "Dummy Endogenous Variables in a Simultaneous Equations System." *Econometrica* 46, 6 (July 1978).
    1979.   "Sample Selection Bias as a Specification Error." *Econometrica* 47, 1 (January 1979).
    1980.   "Sample Selection Bias as a Specification Error: With an Application to the Estimation of Labor Supply Functions." In James P. Smith, ed., *Female Labor Supply: Theory and Estimation*. Princeton, N.J.: Princeton University Press.

Johnson, Norman, and Kotz, Samuel.
    1972.   *Distributions in Statistics: Continuous Multivariate Distributions*. New York: John Wiley.

Kelly, Terrence.
    1976.   "Two Policy Questions Regarding the Minimum Wage." Mimeographed.

Kmenta, Jan.
    1971.   *Elements of Econometrics*. New York: Macmillan.

Kneese, Alan, and Schultze, Charles.
    1975.   *Pollution, Prices and Public Policy*. Washington, D.C.: Brookings Institution.

Landes, Elizabeth.
    1980.   "The Effect of State Maximum Hours Laws on the Employment of Women in 1920." *Journal of Political Economy* 88, 3 (June 1980).

Lee, Lung-fei.
    1978.   "Unionism and Wage Rates: A Simultaneous Equations Model with Qualitative and Limited Dependent Variables." *International Economic Review* 19, 2 (June 1978).

Lester, Richard.
    1967.   "Benefits as a Preferred Form of Compensation." *Southern Economic Journal* 33, 4 (April 1967).

Medoff, James.
    1979.   "Layoffs and Alternatives under Trade Unions in U.S. Manufacturing." *American Economic Review* 69, 3 (June 1979).

Nixon, J. Wilson.
    1975.   "The Minimum Wage and the Job Package." Bureau of Labor Statistics Working Paper No. 32. Washington, D.C.: Bureau of Labor Statistics.

National Board for Prices and Incomes.
    1970.   *Hours of Work, Overtime and Shiftwork.* Report No. 161. London.

Nussbaum, Joyce, and Wise, Donald.
    1977.   "The Employment Impact of the Overtime Provisions of the F.L.S.A." Final report, U.S. Department of Labor Contract J-9-E-6-0105.
    1978.   "The Overtime Pay Premium and Employment." In *Work Time and Employment.* Special Report No. 28. Washington, D.C.: National Commission for Employment Policy.

Oi, Walter.
    1962.   "Labor as a Quasi-Fixed Factor of Production." *Journal of Political Economy* 70, 6 (December 1962).

Paulsen, George E.
    1959.   "The Legislative History of the Fair Labor Standards Act." Ph.D. dissertation, Ohio State University.

Perloff, Jeffrey, and Wachter, Michael.
    1978.   "Work Sharing, Unemployment, and the Rate of Economic Growth." In *Work Time and Employment.* Special

Report No. 28. Washington, D.C.: National Commission for Employment Policy.

Phelps, Orme.
1939. *The Legislative Background of the Fair Labor Standards Act.* Chicago: University of Chicago Press.
1950. *Introduction to Labor Economics.* New York: McGraw-Hill.

Poirer, Dale.
1980. "Partial Observability in Bivariate Probit Models." *Journal of Econometrics* 12, 2 (February 1980).

Quinn, Robert, and Staines, Graham.
1979. *The 1977 Quality of Employment Survey: Descriptive Statistics.* Ann Arbor, Mich.: Survey Research Center, Institute for Social Research, University of Michigan.

Rosen, Sherwin.
1968. "Short-Run Employment Variations in Class I Railroads." *Econometrica* 36, 3–4 (July–October 1968).
1978. "The Supply of Work Schedules and Employment." In *Work Time and Employment.* Special Report No. 28. Washington, D.C.: National Commission for Employment Policy.

Rosenfeld, Carl.
1979. "Multiple Jobholding Holds Steady in 1978." *Monthly Labor Review* 102, 2 (February 1979).

Settle, Russell F., and Weisbrod, Burton.
1978. "Governmentally Imposed Standards: Some Normative Aspects." In Ronald Ehrenberg, ed., *Research in Labor Economics,* vol. 2. Greenwich, Conn.: JAI Press.

Shishko, Robert, and Rostker, Bernard.
1976. "The Economics of Multiple Job Holding." *American Economic Review* 66, 3 (June 1976).

Smith, Robert S.
1976. *The Occupational Safety and Health Act: Its Goals and Achievements.* Washington, D.C.: American Enterprise Institute.
1979. "Compensating Wage Differentials and Public Policy: A Review." *Industrial and Labor Relations Review* 32, 3 (April 1979).

Solnick, Loren, and Swimmer, Gene.
1978. "Overtime and Fringe Benefits—A Simultaneous Equations Approach." Mimeographed.

Stamas, George D.
    1979.   "Long Hours and Premium Pay, May 1978." *Monthly
             Labor Review* 102, 5 (May 1979).
Thaler, Richard, and Rosen, Sherwin.
    1975.   "The Value of Saving a Life: Evidence from the La-
             bor Market." In Nester Terleckyj, ed., *Household Pro-
             duction and Consumption.* New York: National Bureau
             of Economic Research.
Tobin, James.
    1958.   "Estimation of Relationships for Limited Dependent
             Variables." *Econometrica* 26, 1 (January 1958).
U.S., Department of Commerce.
             Fringe Benefits, various issues.
             Employee Benefits, various issues.
U.S., Department of Commerce, Bureau of the Census.
    1978.   *Current Population Survey,* May 1978. (Machine-read-
             able data file). Conducted by the Bureau of the Cen-
             sus for the Bureau of Labor Statistics, Washington,
             D.C.
    1980a.   *1977 Census of Retail Trade: Establishment and Firm Size.*
             Vol. RC77-S-1. Washington, D.C.
    1980b.   *1977 Census of Service Industries: Establishment and Firm
             Size.* Vol. SC77-S-1. Washington, D.C.
U.S., Department of Commerce, Bureau of Economic Analysis.
    1975.   *Business Statistics, 1975.* Washington, D.C.
    1979.   *Survey of Current Business.* Washington, D.C.
U.S., Department of Labor.
    1967.   *Growth of Labor Laws in the United States.* Washington,
             D.C.
    1979.   *1979 Employment and Training Report of the President.*
             Washington, D.C.
U.S., Department of Labor, Bureau of Labor Statistics.
    1973.   *1973 Handbook of Labor Statistics.* Washington, D.C.
    1977.   *1977 Handbook of Labor Statistics.* Washington, D.C.
    1979.   *Characteristics of Major Collective Bargaining Agreements,
             July 1, 1976.* Bulletin 201. Washington, D.C.
U.S., Department of Labor, Employment Standards Administration.
    1967.   *Premium Payments for Overtime under the Fair Labor Stan-
             dards Act.*
    1979.   *Minimum Wage and Maximum Hours Standards under the
             Fair Labor Standards Act, 1978.* Washington, D.C.

U.S., Department of Labor, Wages and Hours and Public Contracts Division.

    1966. *Compliance Survey, 1965*. Washington, D.C.

U.S., House of Representatives.

    1980. *Hearings before the Subcommittee on Labor Standards on HR 1784*. Washington, D.C.: GPO.

Van Atta, Susan.

    1967. "An Analysis of Overtime Hours for Production Workers in Manufacturing Industries, 1957–1965." Ph.D. dissertation, University of California at Berkeley.

Wessels, Walter.

    1980. "The Effects of Minimum Wages in the Presence of Fringe Benefits: An Expanded Model." *Economic Inquiry* 18, 2 (April 1980).